Exiting Indoc

Exiting Indochina

*U.S. Leadership of the Cambodia Settlement
& Normalization of Relations with Vietnam*

Richard H. Solomon

Foreword by Stanley Karnow

UNITED STATES INSTITUTE OF PEACE PRESS
Washington, D.C.

UNITED STATES INSTITUTE OF PEACE
1200 17th Street NW, Suite 200
Washington, DC 20036-3011

First published 2000

Printed in the United States of America

The paper used in this publication meets the minimum requirements of American National Standard for Information Sciences—Permanence of Paper for Printed Library Materials, ANSI Z39.48-1984.

Library of Congress Cataloging-in-Publication Data
Solomon, Richard H., 1937–
　　Exiting Indochina: U.S. leadership of the Cambodia settlement & normalization of relations with Vietnam / Richard H. Solomon; foreword by Stanley Karnow.
　　　　p. cm.
　　Includes bibliographical references and index.
　　ISBN 1-929223-01-3 (alk. paper)
　　1. United States—Foreign relations—Cambodia. 2. Cambodia—Foreign relations—United States. 3. United States—Foreign relations—Vietnam. 4. Vietnam—Foreign relations—United States. 5. United States—Foreign relations—1945–1989. 6. Vietnamese Conflict, 1961–1975—Peace. 7. Vietnamese Conflict, 1961–1965—Cambodia. 8. Cambodia—Politics and government—1979– I. Title.

E183.8.C15 S66 2000
327.73059'09'049—dc21

00-023466

Contents

Foreword

Stanley Karnow

On July 8, 1959, I was visiting Saigon as a correspondent for *Time* magazine when communist guerrillas attacked Bien Hoa, a South Vietnamese
army camp about twenty-five miles north of the city, killing two U.S.
military advisers—Major Dale R. Buis and Master Sergeant Chester M.
Ovnand. My report on the episode was given only a few paragraphs in
the magazine; at the time it deserved no more. It seemed inconceivable to
me at that juncture that I was witnessing the start of a war in which
3 million Americans would ultimately serve, or that the names of Buis
and Ovnand would one day head the list of nearly 60,000 other fatalities
engraved on the black marble of the poignant Vietnam Veterans Memo-
rial in Washington. Nor, as I surveyed the bullet-pocked scene at Bien
Hoa, could I even remotely envision that the conflict would spread, over
the next sixteen years, beyond the borders of Vietnam into adjacent Cambodia and Laos, convulsing those lands and claiming the lives of at least
10 million men, women, and children, both soldiers and civilians.

Stanley Karnow, author and journalist, covered both the French and American wars in
Indochina. Among his several books on Asia is the Pulitzer Prize–winning study *Vietnam:
A History* (New York: Penguin Books, 1997).

In *Exiting Indochina,* Richard Solomon focuses on the aftermath of the Vietnam tragedy as the major powers grappled with the staggering challenge of restoring a measure of stability to the benighted Indochina region. In his position as assistant secretary of state for East Asian and Pacific affairs, he was intimately engaged in the endeavor of negotiating a political resolution to the differences that continued to divide the parties to this enduring conflict. This book, which contains previously unpublished details of the negotiations that led to a United Nations peace plan for Cambodia and the process of normalizing U.S.-Vietnam relations, vividly describes and analyzes the obstacles that constantly thwarted and frequently appeared to propel the task toward disaster.

It was a negotiation immensely complicated by the fact that each of the participants in the process approached the enterprise with its own agenda. The Soviet Union, preoccupied by grave dilemmas at home, in the late 1980s had ceased to provide the Vietnamese with the crucial assistance it had granted them since the end of the war against the Americans and in the subsequent conflict with the Chinese. As a consequence, the Vietnamese economy was deteriorating, in large part because of the huge costs the Vietnamese had incurred in their invasion and occupation of Cambodia in late 1978—a move they had undertaken to overthrow the Khmer Rouge, whom they considered to be China's surrogate in a scheme to encircle them. The Chinese, striving to obstruct Vietnam's hopes to extend its sway over the states of former French Indochina—Laos and Cambodia—were in turn aiding the Khmer Rouge with weapons, sanctuaries, and money, primarily through Thailand. Increasingly isolated and desperate to counterbalance what it viewed as a threat to its security, the Hanoi regime was seeking to normalize its relationship with the United States. But that effort was inhibited by a potent American political lobby, which refused to countenance a U.S.-Vietnam rapprochement until Hanoi accounted for the remains of all the U.S. troops still missing in action from the war of the 1960s and 1970s.

Further compounding this diplomatic tangle, the French continued to nurture their grandiose dream of reestablishing influence in their onetime imperial possession, while the British lacked the dynamism and the resources to play a significant role in Southeast Asia.

Despite these hurdles, the political maneuvering eventually yielded an accommodation. It partly stemmed from the desire of regional states like Australia, Indonesia, Thailand, and Japan to achieve a solution, but mainly it resulted from a secret transaction between China and Vietnam to reconcile their differences within the framework of a United Nations peace plan for Cambodia.

As Solomon notes, it was ironic that the United States, given its deep involvement in the Vietnam War, should emerge as the catalyzing power in the tortuous attempt to reach a diplomatic settlement. What made this possible, he suggests, is that the other parties judged the United States to be the most "neutral" of the major powers in the diplomacy of the early 1990s, and hence able to act as an intermediary in constructing a UN Security Council peace process. Thus America's strategy, which throughout the 1980s had focused primarily on preventing Vietnam from consolidating its influence over Cambodia, shifted to constructing an exit from Indochina for all the major powers—thus transforming the United States from a protagonist into an arbiter.

The devastating Indochina drama—from the 1950s through four subsequent decades of war, revolution, and diplomacy—is a story of grievous misperceptions and miscalculations. It originated in the period following World War II when Western leaders constructed their foreign policies on the assumption that communism was a monolithic global movement controlled by the Kremlin. The concept spawned such dogmas as the "domino theory," which maintained that the fall of one country in Indochina to communism would automatically touch off a chain reaction, causing others throughout Southeast Asia to collapse like a row of wobbly tiles. The bulk of evidence indicated, however, that this facile notion was at best an exaggeration born of fears of an expansionist Soviet Union and revolutionary China. Many communists in the Third World dutifully echoed Soviet or Chinese propaganda, but they were also nationalists whose priorities did not always coincide with those of the Kremlin or the Forbidden City. As intelligence experts knew, some often balked at obeying Moscow's or Beijing's dictates.

The Vietnamese leader Ho Chi Minh was a case in point. As a youth he had been inspired by the lofty French principles of *liberté, égalité, et fraternité*, but was denied the right to practice them by the colonial power. Frustrated, he came to dedicate his life to a single purpose—winning independence for Vietnam. Persuaded that the Soviet Union would promote his crusade, Ho became a professional communist agent. Or, as he later explained, "I was motivated by nationalism rather than ideology." Essentially a pragmatist, Ho explored various routes to reaching his goal. He wrote several letters to Harry Truman requesting support, but the president, to induce the French to concede to the rearmament of West Germany, instead backed Paris's drive to reestablish its colonial administration in Vietnam. In 1950, when Ho founded his government in the jungle, he solicited and obtained recognition from Marshal Tito of Yugoslavia, who was then an apostate in the eyes of Joseph Stalin. For a brief moment, U.S. specialists mused that Ho might not be a Soviet pawn after all, but then dropped the matter. The French, with American support, fought Ho's ragtag forces for eight years and were finally vanquished at the showdown battle of Dien Bien Phu in the spring of 1954. President Eisenhower rejected an appeal from Paris to intervene to rescue the beleaguered French garrisons, having heeded the counsel of his Joint Chiefs of Staff that "Indochina is devoid of any decisive military objective," and that a commitment there would be "a serious diversion of limited U.S. capabilities."

Until that stage a local crisis, Indochina became an international responsibility in May 1954, when the big powers convened at Geneva to negotiate an armistice. The Soviet Union and China, eager to improve their ties with the West, exerted pressure on their Vietnamese comrades to compromise by acquiescing to the partition of Vietnam into northern and southern zones pending nationwide elections scheduled for 1956 to determine which side would govern the country. Ho's prestige after routing the French was unparalleled, and his candidates would have certainly triumphed, but the election was never held. Profoundly disappointed, the traditionally chauvinistic Vietnamese would henceforth distrust foreign intrusions into their problems even more than ever. Years later, obliquely impugning his own allies, North Vietnam's prime minister, Pham Van Dong, bitterly confided to me, "We were betrayed."

Their aspirations to unify Vietnam under their control foiled, the Vietnamese communists gradually launched the struggle that would engulf the United States in the longest war of its history—and culminate in its first military defeat. It is tempting to speculate on how events would have unfolded had diplomacy of the brand pursued by Richard Solomon and his colleagues had been given a chance two generations ago. My opinion is that one of the worst catastrophes of the century might have been averted.

Preface

The long, twilight struggle of the Cold War may have ended without the dreaded nuclear Armageddon between the superpowers, but the global confrontation between the communist world and the democracies did have its hot conflicts. Many of the "small" wars of the second half of the twentieth century were conflicts in the Middle East, Africa, and Asia in which "Third World" allies of the Soviet Union and/or China on the one hand, and the United States and its allies on the other hand, played out revolutionary-nationalist struggles with support from their backers among the major powers.

Two of these surrogate conflicts of the Cold War era, in Asia, drew the United States into costly and frustrating wars that have left as much an imprint on American foreign policy as has the nuclear standoff. The Korean War, 1950–1953, ended in a stalemate between forces of the Republic of Korea and the United States and those of North Korea (Democratic People's Republic of Korea) and Chinese "volunteers"—a standoff that persists today, almost five decades after the end of all-out warfare.

The other hot war of the Cold War years in Asia was the conflict in Indochina—as the French of the colonial era called the three states of Vietnam, Cambodia, and Laos that abut China's southern frontier. America's "Vietnam War," which spilled over to engulf neighboring Cambodia and Laos, followed a century of French colonial domination of the area, Japanese invasion during World War II, and France's defeat by Vietnam's communist revolutionaries in 1954. Between 1955, when

American military advisers were first deployed in South Vietnam (Republic of Vietnam), and 1973, when U.S. forces withdrew under the terms of a peace agreement negotiated with North Vietnam at Paris,[1] the United States waged a drawn-out, bloody, and frustrating conflict against communist guerrilla armies. That struggle ended in defeat for the United States and its South Vietnamese ally. The war claimed more than 58,000 American lives and more than 2 million for the Vietnamese both North and South. The conflict also generated a regionwide cauldron of instability and violence as the North Vietnamese extended supply lines through Laos and Cambodia into South Vietnam, leading U.S. forces to bomb logistical targets in these countries lest they become sanctuaries for North Vietnam's forces.

Two years after the withdrawal of the American military from South Vietnam in 1973, North Vietnam's regular armies conquered all of the south; and in neighboring Cambodia, an indigenous communist revolutionary force known in the West as the Khmer Rouge (Red Khmer) overthrew the pro-U.S. government of the Republic of Cambodia. But Cambodia's travails were not yet over. The country endured fifteen more years of political violence and warfare as, first, the victorious Khmer Rouge promoted a domestic social revolution that took the lives of more than a million Khmer in a spasm of auto-genocidal killing, and then in late 1978, Vietnam invaded and occupied the country, driving the Khmer Rouge from power and establishing a friendly government. (For a discussion of the terms "Cambodia" and "Khmer," see note 5 on page 14 below.)

For Americans, the Vietnam War, our first military defeat abroad, became and persists as a symbol of the unwanted responsibilities and unacceptable costs of international leadership. The political turmoil in the United States stimulated by the Vietnam War produced a great generational divide in American politics. The rallying cry "no more Vietnams" continues to be invoked with each international conflict that threatens to

---

1. See Henry Kissinger, *White House Years* (Boston: Little, Brown, 1979), chapters 8 and 12; and *Years of Upheaval* (Boston: Little, Brown, 1982), chapter 8.

enmesh the United States in warfare abroad. The insistence of our political leaders, especially those in Congress, that any engagement be accompanied by a clearly defined "exit strategy" bespeaks the popular aversion to entrapment in drawn-out and costly conflicts.

In the fullness of time, foreign affairs analysts of another generation may come to see the Vietnam War—as with the Korean conflict—as a necessary, if costly and poorly conceived, battle in the global struggle of the Cold War. For those who lived through the searing domestic and international conflicts of that era, however, "getting out of Vietnam" in 1973 brought to most Americans the liberating lift of escaping a quagmire.

What is less evident to all but the most specialized of observers of U.S. foreign affairs is that America's final exit from the turmoils of Indochina did not occur until two decades after the last U.S. soldiers were evacuated from the roof of the American embassy in Saigon (now Ho Chi Minh City) on April 29, 1973. Two more phases of conflict followed the collapse of the Republic of Vietnam in 1975: the Cambodian revolution and a decade of Vietnamese occupation of that country. Only at the end of the 1980s did the impending collapse of the Soviet Union, in combination with China's persistent pressures on its former ally Vietnam, create the conditions that enabled the United States, and the other major powers, to negotiate a settlement of the Cambodia conflict, enabling them all to withdraw from the region.

This study recounts the diplomacy that brought an end to great power involvement in Indochina, a major cockpit of the Cold War struggles among the United States and its allies, the Soviet Union, and China. The author was an official of the United States government during the years 1989–92. In that capacity he participated in, first, efforts by France and Indonesia to construct a negotiated settlement of the enduring conflict in Cambodia, then an American-catalyzed effort through the United Nations Security Council to negotiate a peace process for Cambodia, and, finally, the construction of a "road map" to normalizing U.S.-Vietnam relations. The history of this diplomacy is worth recording if for no other reason than it documents the final phase of America's decades of involvement in Indochina of the Cold War era.

Another reason for exploring this history is that it highlights the changing character of diplomacy at an important "break point" in international politics. The diplomacy of the Cambodia peace process straddles the years in which the Soviet Union collapsed. As that process reached its climax in the early 1990s, associated conflicts of the Cold War era—the Sino-Soviet confrontation and China's conflict with Vietnam over the two countries' influence in Indochina—became manageable by political processes. Thus, the diplomacy of the Cambodia settlement and U.S.-Vietnam normalization provides a window on an era in which military confrontations and war gave way, perhaps for only a brief time, to an era of political management of international conflicts. How long this era will last is an interesting, if incalculable, matter. What is assessed here is the role of the United States as one among a number of parties to a successful multilateral international mediation effort and its leadership in catalyzing a UN-managed peace process.

It was from this perspective that the author was requested to document his involvement in the diplomacy of the Cambodia peace process. That assessment was published by the United States Institute of Peace in 1999 as a vehicle for teaching and training practitioners in the skills and complexities of international mediation.[2] The present study is an exploration of the process of great power disengagement from Indochina that goes beyond the diplomacy of the Cambodia settlement to recount efforts in the early 1990s to reactivate a process of normalizing U.S.-Vietnam relations.

---

2. See Chester A. Crocker, Fen Osler Hampson, and Pamela Aall, eds., *Herding Cats: Multiparty Mediation in a Complex World* (Washington, D.C.: United States Institute of Peace Press, 1999).

Acknowledgments

In preparing this retrospective history and assessment, the author had significant research support from James Rae. Over the years he also received helpful inputs from a number of colleagues regarding the history of the Indochina conflicts, the Cambodia negotiating effort, and the process of U.S.-Vietnam normalization: Morton Abramowitz, Elizabeth Becker, John Bolton, Frederick Z. Brown, Nayan Chanda, Richard Childress, Gareth Evans, Karl Jackson, Stanley Karnow, Robert Kimmit, Masaharu Kohno, Robert Manning, Claude Martin, Thomas Pickering, Steve Pieczenik, Kenneth Quinn, Brent Scowcroft, Sichan Siv, Stephen Solarz, and Paul Wolfowitz. He alone, however, is responsible for the interpretations developed in this retrospective assessment, as well for any errors of fact.

It should be added that the interpretation developed here is from an American perspective, with the objective of assessing how the United States can play a more effective role in multilateral international efforts to mediate settlements of violent conflicts. The history of these events is so complex that other observers, particularly those from other countries involved in the diplomacy of the Cambodia peace process, would almost certainly give different weights to the roles that various countries played in the process and perhaps have a different interpretation of certain events—à la Akira Kurosawa's classic 1950 film *Rashomon*.

Abbreviations

APEC	Asia Pacific Economic Cooperation forum
ASEAN	Association of Southeast Asian Nations
CGDK	Coalition Government of Democratic Kampuchea
CNN	Cable News Network
CPP	Cambodian People's Party
CSCA	Conference on Security and Cooperation in Asia
DK	Democratic Kampuchea
FUNCINPEC	United National Front for an Independent, Neutral, Peaceful and Cooperative Cambodia
JIM	Jakarta Informal Meetings
KPNLF	Khmer People's National Liberation Front
KPRP	Kampuchean People's Revolutionary Party
KR	Khmer Rouge (see PDK)
Perm Five (P-5)	The five permanent members of the United Nations Security Council: China, France, Great Britain, the Soviet Union (now Russia), and the United States
PDK	Party of Democratic Kampuchea (aka Khmer Rouge)
POW/MIA	Prisoner of War/Missing in Action
PRK	People's Republic of Kampuchea
SNC	Supreme National Council
SOC	State of Cambodia

UN   United Nations

UNTAC   United Nations Transitional Authority in Cambodia

Exiting Indochina

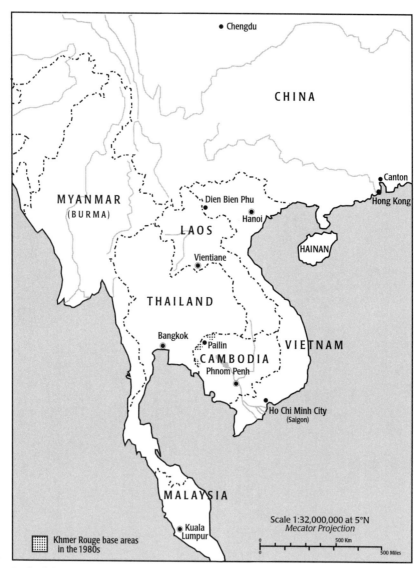

Indochina

Introduction

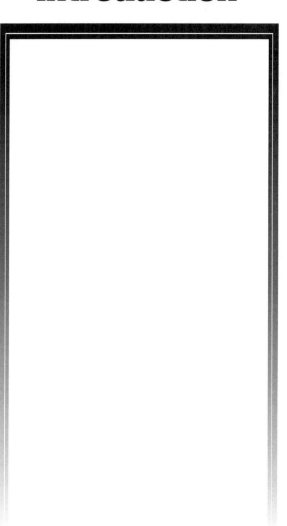

The years 1990–93 marked the phasing out of more than a century of great power interventions in Indochina. The vehicle for this disengagement was the first fully cooperative effort of the United Nations Security Council, as the Cold War was ending, to construct and implement a peace process intended to stabilize a region that had been devastated by conflicts among the major powers and their surrogates. The focus of this diplomacy was Cambodia, a country ravaged for more than two decades by the Vietnam War and internal revolution. The United States played a leading, catalytic role in moving the five permanent members of the Security Council in 1990 to design a political process that would bring peace to Cambodia. Its efforts succeeded because the situation was ripe for a settlement. The combined effects of a military stalemate among Cambodia's political factions, diplomatic efforts to construct a settlement during the preceding decade by a number of interested parties, and the desire of the major powers to disengage from Indochina's travails created a context for successful diplomacy.

The efforts of the United States and the other permanent members of the UN Security Council were reinforced by the diplomacy of several regional states. Indonesia, Thailand, Australia, and Japan were working to eliminate foreign intervention from Indochina and stabilize Southeast Asia, which was feeling the effects of refugee flows resulting from unresolved conflicts affecting Vietnam and Cambodia. Ultimately, success came when the two major protagonists in the region's conflicts of the 1980s and 1990s—China and Vietnam—made a secret, bilateral deal to reconcile their differences and support the United Nations peace plan for Cambodia.

It is ironic that the United States was the most effective of the major powers to move the peace process forward, given the history of its involvement in the Vietnam War. But in the early 1990s the United States was seen by most of the other players as the most "neutral" member of the Security Council, with the political influence and resources to help structure a settlement. The Soviets/Russians and Chinese were still sparring over their influence in Indochina through local surrogates—the Hun Sen government in Phnom Penh and Pol Pot's Khmer Rouge guerrillas in

Cambodia's jungles. Moscow's influence was declining rapidly, however, as a great domestic economic and political crisis contracted its resources and diplomatic outreach. The French, while a prime mover at one stage in the diplomatic maneuvering, were seen as a player with an agenda: seeking to restore their colonial-era influence in both Vietnam and Cambodia. The British, although skilled in UN diplomacy, lacked the political will and the economic strength to be a major influence in Southeast Asia.

The Association of Southeast Asian Nations (ASEAN), led by Indonesia, had laid the basis for a settlement by hosting a series of "prenegotiation" encounters termed the Jakarta Informal Meetings (or JIM meetings) in 1988–89. In the spring of 1989 Indonesia joined forces with France to sponsor an international conference in Paris dedicated to achieving a comprehensive settlement of the Cambodian conflict. This effort foundered on unresolved differences between China and Vietnam and their surrogates among the Khmer factions, but the conference helped to build an international consensus on the elements of a peace process. The Paris Conference put a settlement within reach.

In the early fall of 1989 the Bush administration, at once impelled and constrained by domestic political cross pressures, initiated consultations with the five permanent members of the UN Security Council on a Cambodia settlement. The effort was intended to build on the decade-long series of UN- and ASEAN-sponsored diplomatic efforts and on the Paris Conference accomplishments. This initiative, and a structured process of normalizing U.S.-Vietnam relations that grew from it, ultimately succeeded. Vietnam, increasingly isolated by the rapidly failing Soviet Union and under unrelenting pressure from China, abandoned its objective of establishing a hegemonic position over the other states of Indochina— Laos and Cambodia—and came to terms with China.

By the fall of 1991 a U.S.-brokered Security Council framework agreement for a Cambodia peace process was accepted by all the participants of the Paris Conference of 1989 and formally adopted by the UN General Assembly. In early 1992 the first contingents of the United Nations

Transitional Authority in Cambodia (UNTAC) arrived in Phnom Penh to implement the peace plan.

The United Nations facilitated the U.S. mediation effort. Although the United Nations was, and remains, subject to political attack in the United States, it was a relatively neutral and competent international vehicle for both constructing and implementing a settlement process. The United Nations was not, however, a prime mover in the politics of the settlement; it served as a screen behind which the Chinese, Russians, and Vietnamese privately worked out a resolution of their differences over the future of Indochina. In a series of secret bilateral meetings between senior leaders in Hanoi and Beijing that began in the fall of 1990 and ran through the summer of 1991, the Chinese induced the Vietnamese to accept the UN peace plan for Cambodia. The plan was subsequently formalized by all international participants in the Paris Conference, and by the United Nations, and put into effect in early 1992. The United Nations verified the withdrawal of all Vietnamese troops from Cambodia, UNTAC restored a semblance of civil government in 1992, and in the spring of 1993 the United Nations administered a remarkably successful popular election in Cambodia that established a political structure legitimated by Khmer public opinion. Cambodia was now on its own to run its affairs largely independent of outside interference.

As this process advanced, the United States and Vietnam resumed efforts to normalize relations after the war years and Hanoi's late-1978 invasion of Cambodia. The United States pressed Vietnam to support the UN settlement plan for Cambodia and account for America's missing in action (MIA) in Vietnam and Laos. In 1991 these objectives were formally embodied in a "road map" to normalization that was substantially fulfilled with the establishment of diplomatic relations in July 1995. The United States thus moved beyond its Cold War–era involvement in the strategic and domestic complexities of Indochina to confront the uncertainties and conflicts of the post–Cold War world. For the first time in over a century, Indochina was unburdened of the interventions of the major world powers.

This study describes the U.S. role as one among several players in constructing a peace process for Cambodia, placing the Bush administration's diplomacy in the complex historical and political context of Indochina, the last years of the Cold War, and American domestic politics. It details the evolution of a multilayered settlement process during the years 1989–92 and assesses the outcome of the Cambodian settlement six years after the UN-supervised elections of 1993.

Indochina:
Trapped between
Major Powers

A ny effort to understand the Cambodia peace process must take account of the complex and multifaceted history of Indochina. Virtually all the players in the politics of the early 1990s were burdened with baggage packed with rivalries and conflicts decades if not millennia in the making. The very name Indochina—a French designation of the colonial era—characterizes a region at the geographical boundary between China and the Indian subcontinent, an interstitial zone in world affairs long subject to complex international cross pressures. India and China each imprinted their marks on the culture and politics of the peoples of the region in assertions of power going back millennia.

Of more immediate relevance to this assessment, in the 1800s the French brought European influence to Vietnam and Cambodia in the era of colonialism. Paris placed a teenage Prince Norodom Sihanouk on the Cambodian throne in 1941, in the face of an imminent Japanese invasion of Indochina. Following World War II and France's defeat at the hands of the Vietnamese communists in 1954, Paris sought to regain some of its global outreach by playing a lead role in international diplomacy and reestablishing a presence in Cambodia. Japan, while cautious in its political assertiveness in Asia following the defeat of its imperial ambitions in World War II, was looking to gain greater regional stature in an era of "geoeconomics." Some officials in the Japanese Foreign Ministry, seeking to translate their country's economic power into political influence, even looked anew to a time of "Asia for Asians."[3]

In the 1970s Indochina became a cockpit of the global rivalry between the Soviet Union and China that developed after the breakdown of their alliance in 1960. The two communist giants had supported the Vietnamese in the 1960s during their war with the Americans, but by 1974 Beijing had turned against Hanoi to resist the regional expansion of the victorious

---

3. See Yoichi Funabashi, "The Asianization of Asia," *Foreign Affairs* (November–December 1993): 75–85; and Masaharu Kohno, *In Search of Proactive Diplomacy: Increasing Japan's Diplomatic Role in the 1990s* (Washington, D.C.: Brookings Institution, Center for Northeast Asian Policy Studies, 1999).

Vietnamese, whom the Chinese saw as a surrogate of the Soviet Union in its effort to contain China's influence in Asia.[4] After Vietnam's invasion of Cambodia in late 1978, the Chinese launched a limited border war on the Sino-Vietnamese frontier and supported via Thailand an insurgency against Vietnam's client regime in Phnom Penh—a regime that was also supported by the Soviets.

In Indochina's complex history, the influence of outside powers has long been amplified by regional rivalries and internal political factionalism. The three states of Indochina—Vietnam, Laos, and Cambodia—along with neighboring Thailand and Burma, have a complicated record of interventions and shifting dominations going back centuries. Contemporary Khmer embody this history in an intense distrust and hostility toward the Vietnamese. Fear of Vietnamese "colonialism," in the form of Hanoi's invasion of Cambodia in 1978 and subsequent military occupation, was reinforced by the presence in the country of several hundred thousand Vietnamese settlers. Thai fears of the Vietnamese led Bangkok to cooperate with China and Khmer forces throughout the 1980s to resist the stabilization of a Vietnamese surrogate regime in Phnom Penh. These issues constituted some of the key political factors at play in the peace process of the early 1990s.

America's post–World War II involvement in Indochina grew slowly after the Vietnamese defeat of the French at Dien Bien Phu in 1954. The Sino-Soviet alliance of 1950 projected the Cold War throughout Asia, and the United States sought to prevent states allied to the major communist powers such as North Vietnam and North Korea, or indigenous communist parties in countries like Indonesia, from spreading the influence of Moscow and revolutionary China. In this context, in the 1960s the United States took on the costly and ultimately unsuccessful task of

---

4. As late as 1989, Deng Xiaoping told President Bush that Moscow's relationships with Vietnam and Cambodia were a threat to China because they represented a continuation of Soviet efforts to "encircle" his country going back to the Khrushchev and Brezhnev eras. See George Bush and Brent Scowcroft, *A World Transformed*, 94–96.

thwarting revolutionary nationalism in Vietnam and Cambodia. In 1972 the United States found common cause with China in shared opposition to the expansionist Soviet Union and its allies. After Hanoi's military intervention in Cambodia in 1978, the United States worked alongside China and with Thailand to resist the expansion of Vietnamese influence. The three countries supported anti-Vietnamese Khmer resistance forces based in Thailand, the United States backing noncommunist groups led by Prince Sihanouk and Son Sann, the Chinese and the Thai supporting these same groups but also the Cambodian communist organization known as the Khmer Rouge (Red Khmer). Chinese and Thai support for the Khmer Rouge was to become a major source of tension in the politics of a Cambodia peace process. Yet Washington and Beijing, along with the ASEAN countries, were determined to prevent Hanoi from consolidating its client government in Phnom Penh led by a former Khmer Rouge commander, Hun Sen.

From War
to Diplomacy

The 1950s, 1960s, and 1970s were a time of military efforts—by the French, the Americans, the Chinese, and the Vietnamese—to shape the future of Indochina. In the 1980s international efforts slowly shifted toward diplomacy. Early in the decade concern focused on Vietnam's 1978 invasion of Cambodia and on Hanoi's efforts to gain international recognition of its client government in Phnom Penh led by Heng Samrin and Hun Sen. In the summer of 1980 the Japanese sponsored a small conference in Tokyo designed to build pressure on Vietnam to withdraw its troops from Cambodia; and in July 1981 the United Nations convened an International Conference on Kampuchea (Cambodia) in New York.[5] The UN session, chaired by Austrian foreign minister Willibald Pahr, was attended by ninety-one countries—but not by the Soviet Union or Vietnam. It sought to attain a comprehensive settlement of the Cambodian situation based on the withdrawal of Vietnam's military forces, disarmament of the contending Khmer factions, and the establishment of an interim administration pending national elections for a new Cambodian government.

These issues—a comprehensive (as opposed to a partial) settlement plan under some form of international supervision, withdrawal of Vietnam's troops, disarmament of the Khmer factions, and the establishment of a legitimate government through elections—became the essential elements of diplomatic maneuvering over Cambodia for the ensuing decade. Challenging this political equation was the determination of the Vietnamese, and their Soviet backers, to sustain a government in Phnom Penh friendly to their interests.

The remainder of the 1980s saw fruitless political and military maneuvering among the contending Khmer parties. The UN secretary-general's special representative for Cambodia, Rafeeuddin Ahmed, and the ASEAN

---

5. The early name for Cambodia was Kambuja, pronounced Cambodia by Westerners but Kampuchea by the Khmer. Throughout this study we will use the name Cambodia, except in official designations that use Kampuchea. Khmer is the designation of ethnic Cambodians; we will use both terms—Khmer and Cambodia—as appropriate in this account.

states, led by Indonesia's foreign minister, Ali Alatas, tried without success to establish the basis for a political settlement. Of special importance in these efforts were two "informal" meetings in Jakarta—the JIM meetings—held in 1988 and early 1989. These encounters succeeded to the extent of getting the four Khmer factional leaders together, along with representatives of the other Indochina states and the ASEAN countries. JIMs I and II put on the agenda the issue of some form of international control mechanism to supervise a settlement, but a political process failed to take hold as the Khmer factions continued to test their strength through military action on the ground.

Two other factors began to change the diplomatic equation by the mid-1980s. In the United States, growing awareness of the horrendous violence perpetrated by Pol Pot's Khmer Rouge[6] during its reign of revolutionary terror between 1975 and 1978 weakened support for the anti-Vietnamese coalition of Khmer parties that included the Khmer Rouge, formally termed the Coalition Government of Democratic Kampuchea (CGDK).[7] Of greater significance, the ascension to power in Moscow of Mikhail Gorbachev in 1985 led to a fundamental shift in Soviet foreign policy, away from the expansionist initiatives of the Khrushchev

---

6. The Pol Pot faction of the Cambodian communist movement is commonly referred to as the Khmer Rouge. The movement established a state termed Democratic Kampuchea (DK) after its successful insurgency against the U.S.-sponsored Lon Nol government of the Republic of Cambodia in 1975. After the Vietnamese drove the Pol Pot government out of Phnom Penh in late 1978, the movement renamed itself the Party of Democratic Kampuchea (PDK), and in 1982 it allied itself with the noncommunist forces of Prince Sihanouk and Son Sann under the name of the Coalition Government of Democratic Kampuchea (CGDK).

7. Specialists in Southeast Asian affairs were generally aware of Khmer Rouge violence, which had been first reported in diplomatic channels by a U.S. Foreign Service officer, Kenneth Quinn, as early as 1974. (Quinn was to play a central role in subsequent negotiations in the early 1990s regarding the Cambodia settlement and normalization of relations with Vietnam.) The horrific violence of the Khmer Rouge in power was documented by Elizabeth Becker in *When the War Was Over: Cambodia and the Khmer Rouge Revolution* (New York: Perseus Books, Public Affairs, 1998) and Nayan Chanda in *Brother Enemy: The War after the War* (New York: Collier Books, 1986). The 1984 film *The Killing Fields*, which won three Academy Awards the following year, made the Khmer Rouge revolution a matter of wide public awareness in the United States.

and Brezhnev eras and toward normalization of relations with the United States and China.

In July 1986 Gorbachev gave a major foreign policy speech at Vladivostok on the Soviet Union's Pacific frontier. The presentation publicized the withdrawal of some Soviet troops from Afghanistan and Mongolia, a clear signal of Gorbachev's interest in improving relations with China. The Soviet leadership continued to express support for Vietnam, in part by deferring to Hanoi's regional objectives by speaking of Vietnam, Laos, and Cambodia as if they were a single political entity. Behind the scenes, however, Gorbachev and his foreign minister, Eduard Shevardnadze, were making clear to the Vietnamese that the era of Soviet support for Vietnam in its confrontation with China, including subsidization of the Vietnamese occupation of Cambodia, was fast coming to an end. On April 5, 1989, one month before Gorbachev traveled to Beijing to complete the normalization of Sino-Soviet relations, Vietnam announced that it would withdraw all its forces from Cambodia by the end of September of that year—unilaterally if necessary, under some form of international verification if possible.[8]

---

8. The Vietnamese had announced troop withdrawals in previous years, but these "withdrawals" were assessed to be annual rotational reassignments. In May 1988 Hanoi announced it would withdraw 50,000 troops by the end of the year and place the remaining Vietnamese troops under the command of the Hun Sen government. The April 1989 announcement was the first time Vietnam said it would withdraw *all* its troops from Cambodia.

Constructing a Peace Process for Cambodia

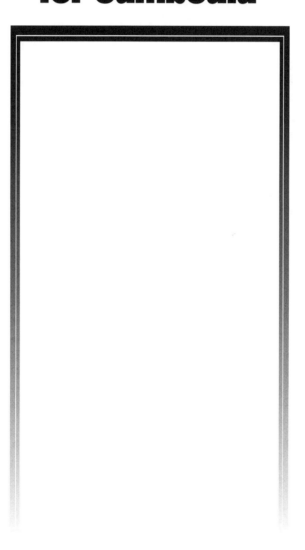

The Vietnamese troop withdrawal announcement reactivated a number of diplomatic efforts to negotiate a political settlement of the Cambodian conflict. The work of constructing a peace process, in all, spanned more than a decade and involved multiple players—primarily the United Nations, ASEAN, and individual countries such as Australia, France, Indonesia, Japan, Thailand, and the United States. The history of this effort rather neatly falls into five distinct phases.

The first phase covered most of the decade of the 1980s and involved the partially successful "prenegotiation" efforts of the United Nations and ASEAN.[9] These initiatives, as already mentioned, helped define the issues relevant to a settlement and brought about the first meetings of the four major Khmer political factions at a negotiating table.[10] As these efforts proceeded, the factions sustained their military confrontation with the support of outside backers: the Chinese and the Thai supporting Prince Sihanouk and Son Sann as well as Pol Pot's Khmer Rouge; the United States and several ASEAN countries supporting Prince Sihanouk and Son Sann; and Vietnam and Moscow backing Hun Sen's Cambodian People's Party (CPP) and its government, the People's Republic of Kampuchea (PRK), a designation changed in 1989 to the State of Cambodia (SOC).

The second phase, from the spring of 1989 through August of that year, centered on the French-Indonesian negotiating effort—formally termed the Paris Conference on Cambodia—which convened in Paris during the month of August.

---

9. See Harold Saunders, "We Need a Larger Theory of Negotiation: The Importance of Pre-negotiating Phases," in *Negotiation Theory and Practice*, ed. J. William Breslin and Jeffrey Z. Rubin (Cambridge, Mass.: Harvard Law School, Program on Negotiation, 1991), 57–70.

10. The four political factions were Prince Sihanouk's United National Front for an Independent, Neutral, Peaceful and Cooperative Cambodia (FUNCINPEC); Son Sann's Khmer People's National Liberation Front (KPNLF); Pol Pot's Party of Democratic Kampuchea (PDK), generally referred to as the Khmer Rouge; and Hun Sen's Cambodian People's Party (the CPP, prior to 1989 known as the Kampuchean People's Revolutionary Party, the KPRP).

The third phase began in the fall of 1989, following suspension of the Paris Conference, and centered around the U.S. initiative to construct a UN peace process through the work of the five permanent members of the Security Council (popularly referred to as the P-5 or Perm Five). It concluded when the Perm Five reached consensus on a framework for the peace process at the end of August 1990.

The fourth phase, which began with Security Council publication of the Perm Five framework agreement on August 28, 1990, ran through the fall of 1991 and involved broadening international backing for the Perm Five framework agreement and, most significantly, gaining the cooperation of the four Khmer political factions.

The fifth phase was the period of implementation of the UN settlement plan. It began in early 1992 with the arrival in Cambodia of UN troops under the supervision of the secretary-general's special representative, Yasushi Akashi; ran through the elections of May 1993; and concluded with the establishment of a new government and withdrawal of the UN presence from Cambodia in September of that year.

U.S. involvement in this five-phase process was most active in the second and third phases: during the first session of the Paris Conference and the subsequent Perm Five negotiations that produced the framework agreement.

I had been publicly nominated as assistant secretary of state for East Asian and Pacific affairs on March 24, 1989, ten days before the Vietnamese announced their intention to fully withdraw their military forces from Cambodia by the end of September.[11] Not long thereafter, I received my first official invitation, from France's Ambassador to Washington,

---

11. Readers may well be jarred by the occasional use of the first person in this account. My excuse for personalizing the narrative is that I was originally asked to reconstruct the history of this period based on my personal involvement in the diplomacy. As well, the circumlocution "the author" sounded to my editorial ear both awkward and even more pretentious than use of the first person.

Emmanuel "Bobby" de Margerie, to a breakfast in honor of my soon-to-be French counterpart, Claude Martin, director of the Quai d'Orsay's Asia-Oceania Division. Martin was coming to Washington specifically to gain U.S. support for the conference on Cambodia that France and Indonesia were planning for August.[12]

The Bush administration, in its first months, had reaffirmed with China its opposition to Vietnam's occupation of Cambodia and its support for the noncommunist resistance. Although the administrations's attitude toward the Khmer Rouge was decidedly unfriendly, it did sustain the policy of supporting the Sihanouk–Son Sann–Khmer Rouge coalition government (the CGDK) as the legitimate incumbent in Cambodia's UN seat. As with the Reagan administration, the policy was intended to block recognition of the Vietnamese-installed government of Hun Sen. The Bush administration also reconsidered the issue of providing assistance—both lethal and humanitarian—to the noncommunist resistance forces of Prince Sihanouk and Son Sann, leader of the Khmer People's National Liberation Front (KPNLF).[13] The rationale for such assistance, which had been first proposed in Congress in 1985 by the chairman of the House of Representatives' Foreign Affairs Subcommittee on Asian and Pacific

---

12. The French-Indonesian initiative was taken at the urging of Prince Sihanouk, who had approached the French early in 1989 and appealed to them to convene a peacemaking conference for his country. The prince was concerned that Hun Sen was consolidating his position as head of an effective government in Phnom Penh, a development that in time would freeze him out of an opportunity to regain leadership in Cambodia. The French initially planned to convene a conference on their own, but after an approach from Indonesian foreign minister Ali Alatas, they decided to make the effort a joint venture with ASEAN—whose support they would need if they were to regain some influence in their former colonies of Cambodia and Vietnam.

13. The issue of U.S. assistance to the noncommunists in the resistance was to become one of the most controversial domestic political issues in developing a settlement plan. Both the Reagan and Bush administrations provided nonlethal humanitarian assistance to FUNCINPEC and the KPNLF and their military forces on a covert basis. They considered but rejected proposals to provide *lethal* military equipment, which was supplied by China and several ASEAN states. In the spring of 1991, under congressional pressure, the Bush administration began several overt humanitarian assistance and economic development–oriented aid programs to the noncommunist resistance and to Hun Sen's State of Cambodia.

Affairs, Stephen J. Solarz, and his Republican colleague Jim Leach, was to strengthen the noncommunist elements in the resistance vis-à-vis the Chinese-backed Khmer Rouge, and to give them more credibility in any negotiation involving the Hun Sen government in Phnom Penh.[14]

The Bush administration was not inclined to take the lead on Indochina issues, however. My official instructions were to support the French and the Indonesians in their preparations for the August conference in Paris. Claude Martin and I had a cordial first encounter at the French embassy; we were to become active collaborators in the months to follow.

The evolution of great power cooperation on a Cambodia settlement was complicated in early June 1989 by the violent events at Tiananmen Square in China's capital, Beijing. Eight days before my confirmation hearings in the U.S. Senate, Chinese troops fired on unarmed pro-democracy demonstrators who had been protesting corruption in the government for several months. The violence was broadcast live and worldwide by CNN. Overnight our official contacts with China became a domestic political liability. In an effort to sustain a policy dialogue with the Chinese leadership, now publicly denigrated as "the butchers of Beijing," President Bush dispatched a secret mission to China in early July that, when revealed to the public at the end of the year, ignited a domestic firestorm of criticism.

Paradoxically, Tiananmen and the worldwide criticism of the Chinese leadership that it evoked heightened Chinese sensitivities about their continuing support for the ruthless Khmer Rouge. The criticism increased Beijing's interest in a political settlement of the Cambodia conflict in a way that would distance China from Pol Pot and his movement. Nonetheless, China's strategic objective remained consonant with that of the

---

14. See *Congressional Record*, 1985, 131, no. 90, sec. 206–207. Neither the Reagan and Bush administrations nor the Congress advocated supplying lethal assistance to the noncommunist resistance. Neither party sought a military solution to the conflict, and all parties calculated that military aid would reactivate some of the international and domestic political tensions of the Vietnam War period.

United States: to prevent Vietnam from establishing hegemony over all of Indochina.[15]

This contradictory mix of public criticism of China and private diplomatic cooperation made for complex relations between the State Department and the American public and Congress. In the months following Tiananmen we collaborated politically with the Chinese in an effort to replace the Hun Sen government with a UN-backed transitional authority headed by Prince Sihanouk and committed to establishing a democratic government in Cambodia. Yet we were attacked in Congress and in public for appearing to support China's strategy of undermining Vietnam's client government in Phnom Penh by building up a resistance coalition that included the dreaded Khmer Rouge.

Our diplomatic objective, in fact, was a settlement that would end Chinese military assistance to Pol Pot's forces and control the Khmer Rouge by way of a substantial UN presence in Cambodia. In terms of domestic American politics, however, it was not clear that the Bush administration could accommodate Beijing's political requirements of including the Khmer Rouge in a transitional Cambodian leadership or give Khmer Rouge leaders the opportunity to run for office in UN-supervised elections. For the Bush administration, squaring this circle was to be the most politically contentious and risk-laden aspect of constructing a peace process.

---

15. There is a long history of efforts by Ho Chi Minh to establish an Indochinese Communist Party as the vehicle for uniting the three states of Indochina under Vietnamese leadership. See MacAlister Brown, "The Indochina Federation Idea: Learning from History," in *Postwar Indochina: Old Enemies and New Allies*, ed. Joseph J. Zasloff (Washington, D.C.: Foreign Service Institute/Department of State, 1988).

Progress at Paris

he American delegation to the Paris Conference on Cambodia departed Washington on July 28, 1989, under the leadership of Secretary of State James A. Baker III. On the plane ride to Paris, Baker briefed the press on U.S. objectives in supporting the French-Indonesian initiative. He said that the administration's goal in supporting ASEAN and the CGDK was to achieve a comprehensive settlement with five elements: an immediate cease-fire and the eventual termination of all foreign military assistance to the Khmer factions; the formation of an interim administration headed by Prince Sihanouk; the establishment of a process that would culminate in the internationally supervised election of a new constitutional government; the voluntary return to Cambodia of the large Khmer refugee population in Thailand; and the creation of an international control mechanism to implement a settlement process, "which we think ought to be a United Nations monitoring force."

Secretary Baker was to involve himself directly in the Cambodia negotiations on four occasions over the coming two years, each time setting a critical parameter of the settlement process. The first of these interventions was at the opening of the Paris Conference, when he established the American position on the scope of an agreement—in the process constraining Vietnam and its supporters in their room for political maneuver.

Before departing for Paris, we had received information that the Vietnamese were trying to build support for a *partial* solution to the Cambodian conflict. They hoped to limit international involvement in a settlement to verification of the withdrawal of their troops, perhaps some oversight of an election, but no arrangement that would weaken the authority of their client regime, the State of Cambodia, and its political structure, the Cambodian People's Party headed by Hun Sen. Thus did Hanoi hope to unburden itself at once of the political stigma and the cost of its military invasion and occupation of the country, while leaving in place a friendly government with broadened international support.

In Paris the Vietnamese delegation, headed by senior diplomat Foreign Minister Nguyen Co Thach, as anticipated, pressed for a partial settlement with the argument that including the Pol Pot faction in a political process risked legitimizing and returning to power genocidal murderers. Thach sought to strengthen the rationale for his position by asserting that only the Hun Sen government, intact, had the power to prevent the dreaded Khmer Rouge from fighting their way back to power. This argument had little resonance among the conference participants, who generally supported the view that the best way to constrain the Khmer Rouge was to give them some stake in a political process subject to international supervision. Vietnam's rationale did elicit some support in the United States and in a few other countries, however, substantially complicating the administration's task of building domestic support for a UN settlement plan that involved a limited and constrained form of inclusion of the Khmer Rouge.

Secretary Baker preemptively took on the issue of a partial settlement at the Paris Conference. At the end of the opening ministerial session, he convened an informal get-together with the conference cochairs, Foreign Ministers Roland Dumas of France and Ali Alatas of Indonesia. In a darkened eating hall of the French Foreign Ministry's elegant Kléber Conference Centre, the secretary told the cochairs that the United States remained firmly committed to achieving a comprehensive settlement and that he did not intend to return to the concluding ministerial session a month later for anything less.

After Baker and most of the other ministers departed the Paris opening, the conference broke into five technical working groups: one to work out the mandate for an international control mechanism to oversee a settlement process (chaired by Canada and India); a second to guarantee Cambodia's sovereignty while committing all parties to the settlement to support its implementation (headed by Laos and Malaysia); a third, chaired by Australia and Japan, to consider the issues of repatriating the more than 350,000 Khmer refugees in Thailand and reconstructing the country.

The fourth group, an ad hoc committee composed of the four Cambodian political factions, was chaired by France and Indonesia. Its mandate was to focus on the most difficult issue of constructing an interim Khmer authority, involving the four factions under Prince Sihanouk's leadership, which would oversee internationally supervised elections during the transition to a new government. A fifth working group, termed the "coordinating committee," was also cochaired by France and Indonesia. It took responsibility for drafting a final conference document for consideration at a concluding ministerial session.[16]

These groups labored on at the Kléber Conference Centre through much of the month of August, enjoying elegant French cuisine and making significant progress on all the assigned issues except the key "internal" matter of a power-sharing arrangement among the four Khmer factions. Hun Sen's delegation, backed by the Vietnamese, resisted any arrangement that would include Pol Pot's Khmer Rouge in the settlement or weaken the standing of the State of Cambodia government in Phnom Penh. The delegation also objected to any substantial role for the United Nations in the transition to elections beyond confirming the withdrawal of Vietnamese forces and monitoring the electoral process. The delegation stressed the danger of the genocidal Khmer Rouge returning to power and the need to sustain the existing government-military structure in Phnom Penh as the only sure counter to a return to power of Pol Pot.

In conference discussions of the human rights of the Khmer people, the Khmer Rouge delegation, headed by Foreign Minister Khieu Samphan, and the Chinese resisted characterization of Khmer Rouge policies and practices during their rule in the 1970s as constituting a "genocide." They stressed the need for a four-party coalition governing authority under Prince Sihanouk's leadership as the only way to restore Cambodia's sovereignty after a decade of "colonial" rule by Vietnam's surrogate regime

---

16. The work of the Paris Conference, and the subsequent UN settlement agreement, is described and assessed in detail in Steven R. Ratner, "The Cambodia Settlement Agreements," *American Journal of International Law* 87, no. 1 (January 1993). Ratner was an attorney-adviser in the Office of the Legal Adviser, U.S. Department of State. He participated in both the Paris Conference and the UN–Perm Five negotiations as a member of the U.S. delegation.

under Hun Sen. They asserted that Vietnam's "colonialism" would be sustained after the withdrawal of Hanoi's troops because of the presence of more than a million ethnic Vietnamese settlers in the country.

By August 20 it was clear to the French that their conference was headed for a deadlock on the "internal" issue of a power-sharing arrangement among the fractious Khmer. In an effort to avoid a diplomatic setback for his government, Claude Martin drafted for limited circulation a "skeleton paper" that sought to break the impending diplomatic impasse. He floated the idea of a power-sharing arrangement that involved maintenance of the State of Cambodia's governmental structure with Hun Sen as prime minister, Sihanouk as president but without authority over the prime minister, and a very constrained, largely symbolic role for the Khmer Rouge. The document made no mention of the United Nations as a control mechanism during the transition to elections or in a peacekeeping mode. Martin pressed Sihanouk and the Chinese to support this arrangement and warned that they would bear the burden of international censure if they did not deliver Khmer Rouge support for it.

Sihanouk was counting on the conference to construct a balance of international and domestic forces that would constrain or neutralize the powers of both the Khmer Rouge and Hun Sen in a way that would give him renewed powers of leadership. He expressed outrage at the exploratory French initiative, which substantially gave the Vietnamese and Hun Sen what they were hoping to achieve in Paris. In a three-hour private meeting with the U.S. delegation at his temporary residence in the Paris suburb of Roissy, the prince ridiculed the French for their impatience to resolve in one month a conflict that had raged for more than a decade. He proposed dismantling both the Hun Sen government and his resistance coalition and in their stead establishing a quadripartite government with himself as president and four vice chairmen, one representing each of the four factions. He also proposed an international control mechanism of some sort to dismantle the factional military forces and their arms caches. This approach, the prince asserted, was the only way to prevent a full-scale civil war in his country.

Sihanouk, as ever trying to position himself as a balancer in the political middle, went on to rail against Hun Sen as a national traitor for collaborating with the Vietnamese; and (for balance) he expressed distrust of China's intentions for their unwavering support of Pol Pot. Only he himself, the prince asserted, was a true nationalist with the moral authority to lead a government of national reconciliation. He confessed that the Khmer factions, by themselves, were incapable of achieving national reconciliation. He needed the support of the international community to structure and enforce a settlement that would prevent Cambodia from succumbing to civil war. Sihanouk made clear to us in private that he would reject the French compromise plan. It was designed, he asserted, to enable France and Indonesia to claim they had at last solved the problem of Cambodia.

With the conference deadlocked, Secretary Baker, the foreign ministers of the Soviet Union, Great Britain, and China, and the UN secretary-general absented themselves from the concluding ministerial meeting, which convened on August 28 amid considerable uncertainty as to the final results of the monthlong negotiation. French foreign minister Dumas, who along with Indonesia's Alatas chaired the concluding session, challenged the delegates to muster the political will to resolve five major issues crystallized by the conference: the role of the United Nations, if any, in a settlement; how to organize and control a cease-fire of the Khmer combatants; how to deal with the issue of Pol Pot's genocide—its past and possible resumption; the matter of the Vietnamese "foreign settlers" in Cambodia; and how to create a process of national reconciliation among the four Khmer factions.

The ensuing discussion among the remaining ministers was remarkably upbeat, as the various delegations stressed all that had been accomplished in the preceding month: consensus on the need for a comprehensive resolution of the conflict; the need for a direct UN role of some sort in a settlement process; a role for the Khmer Rouge in the transition to elections as the best approach to preventing full-blown civil war; the concurrent need for measures to prevent a return to the policies and practices of

Pol Pot's violent regime; and, as the final outcome, the election of a new Cambodian government under UN oversight.

The contributions of the four Cambodian factions to the concluding ministerial meeting were considerably less elevated. Indeed, they reinforced the political deadlock. Hun Sen stressed the need to explicitly mention Pol Pot's "genocide" in a final document (rather than use the oblique and convoluted phrase "the universally condemned policies and practices of a recent past," which conference participants had designed to bring the Khmer Rouge into the political process) and the need to maintain his government intact until after elections. Vietnam's Thach seconded Hun Sen on the issue of genocide, saying his country would never sign an agreement that legalized the Khmer Rouge. He added that he was prepared to accept a role for the United Nations in a settlement process if Cambodia's UN seat, occupied since 1979 by the Khmer Rouge (and after 1982 by their coalition partners in the CGDK), was vacated. Khieu Samphan made a brief intervention that stressed the indispensability of Sihanouk's leadership, the need to get all Vietnamese forces out of Cambodia under UN supervision, and the provocative proposal of either eliminating all the factional armies or cutting them back to equal size.

The performance of the hour was Sihanouk's. Appearing haggard and somewhat disoriented because of sleepless nights in anticipation of a failed conference, the prince asserted his position as the sole guarantor of Cambodia's sovereignty. "Because of destiny I was placed at the head of Cambodia at the age of $18\frac{1}{2}$. At 68, at the end of my life, I'm not about to become a traitor" (by accepting Vietnamese domination of the country via Hun Sen's regime). He went on to assert the need for a quadripartite government that would correspond to the realities of contemporary Cambodia. "I'm for genocide [the Khmer Rouge]," he blurted out. "No, no! Of course I'm *against* genocide, but I'm also against colonialism. Hun Sen must join in a four-party coalition so that the Cambodian people can exercise their sovereignty through elections. If Hun Sen is certain that he will get 80 percent of the vote, why does he fear elections?" taunted the prince. "If he wins, he can state that Cambodia belongs to the club of the three Indochina communist states."

Giving balance to his attack, Sihanouk asserted he was not a spokesman for the Khmer Rouge, "the torturers of my family." He was prepared to speak out against Pol Pot and his genocide and of the need to protect human rights, but in the interest of a settlement based on a four-party transitional government he would agree to withdraw the word "genocide" from the conference document. The one issue on which he did not comment was the role of the United Nations in a settlement.

How to end the conference? It was deadlocked by the standoff between the Khmer opponents of Pol Pot's "genocide" and the Khmer who opposed the "colonialism" of Vietnam's surrogate regime; and behind the factions lurked the continuing confrontation between Beijing and Hanoi over the future of Indochina. Rather than declare failure, the French and Indonesian organizers "suspended" the monthlong session. "It is not yet possible to achieve a comprehensive settlement," noted the final conference communiqué. The cochairs urged all the conference participants to intensify their efforts to reach a settlement, declaring that they would begin consultations within six months with a view to reconvening the conference in Paris.

In fact, efforts were already under way to pursue other routes to a settlement. Thai prime minister Chatichai Choonhavan was preparing to initiate from Bangkok an effort at "shuttle diplomacy" among the four Khmer factions with the goal of achieving, as a first step, a cease-fire.[17] (Chatichai's effort, as it unfolded, was to split his government and fail in its purpose.) Sihanouk, alienated by French pressures to side with Hun Sen, was also looking for a solution based on regional diplomacy. Rather than return to the Paris Conference, the prince was talking to the Thai about a new round of talks based either in Bangkok or Phuket involving the UN

---

17. See Steven Erlanger, "Thai Leader Trying to Break Cambodian Impasse," *New York Times*, September 11, 1989.

Security Council's five permanent members, the six ASEAN states, the Lao, the Vietnamese, and the four Khmer factions. At the same time, Indonesian foreign minister Alatas, leader of ASEAN's initiatives on Cambodia, the Japanese, and the Australians were each beginning to conceptualize their own follow-on efforts.

Meanwhile, on the ground in Cambodia, the Khmer Rouge, the KPNLF, and Hun Sen's State of Cambodia were launching new tests of military strength.

The United States Initiates a UN-Centered Effort

The Paris Conference had had an ambiguous outcome regarding a role for the United Nations in a peace process; some proposed it, a few opposed it. The idea of a settlement with significant United Nations involvement had been discussed informally for some time. In April 1989, U.S. congressman Stephen Solarz had had a long discussion with Sihanouk's son, Prince Ranarridh, at the FUNCINPEC refugee camp— "Site B"—along the Thai-Cambodian border about strategies for ending his country's travails. Solarz raised the possibility of establishing a UN trusteeship over Cambodia as a way of working around the inability of the Khmer factions to establish a process of national reconciliation.[18] Ranarridh was attracted to the idea. Although Article 78 of the United Nations Charter precludes a member state from reverting back to the status of a UN trust territory, it seemed clear that the United Nations was the only institution that might bring the weight of the international community to bear on the irreconcilable Khmer political factions.

After returning from Paris at the end of August, I instructed the legal experts and Cambodia specialists in our delegation to prepare a strategy for building on the results of the Paris Conference through a UN-centered initiative. By the time the General Assembly convened for its forty-fourth annual session a month later, we had prepared Secretary of State Baker to launch his second key intervention in the increasingly roiled diplomatic waters of a Cambodia settlement.

At the annual breakfast meeting between the ASEAN foreign ministers and the secretary of state at New York's Waldorf Astoria Hotel on September 29, Secretary Baker informed the ministers that, in view of the suspension of the Paris Conference, he believed the time had come for the UN Security Council to "lay its hands" on the issue of a Cambodia settlement. The challenge, said Baker, was to prevent "the dialogue of diplomacy from being replaced by the dialogue of the battlefield." During the next three months, planning advanced within the State

---

18. See Becker, *When the War Was Over*, 393.

Department for a Cambodia peace process premised on "an enhanced role for the United Nations."

The policy judgments that shaped the U.S. role in the ensuing diplomacy are important to describe, for they became the focus of intense domestic political attack and some international challenge. Secretary Baker had said to the press on his way to the Paris Conference the preceding July that the United States had several fundamental objectives in structuring a comprehensive political settlement: to enable Cambodia to regain its sovereign national independence (that is, to see it break out of Hanoi's sphere of influence); to establish a democratic domestic political order though elections; and to prevent the Khmer Rouge from regaining control over the country.

Given the experience of the Paris Conference, we had come to the conclusion that the most promising approach to achieving these goals was through a major role for the United Nations in a transition to elections. An impartial body with international authority and significant resources was needed to control or dismantle the factional military forces, administer the institutions of civil authority, organize elections, deal with reconstruction issues such as the repatriation of Khmer refugees in Thailand, promote economic development, and protect the human rights of the population. We also believed that Prince Sihanouk—however "mercurial"—was an essential political factor in constructing such a settlement.[19]

---

19. The matter of Sihanouk's role in a settlement process was an issue of some contention. Certain American observers of the Cambodian scene, and several congressmen, believed that Sihanouk's past association with the Khmer Rouge compromised his credibility as a political leader. Others felt that his well-deserved reputation for "mercurial" political maneuvering, which included periods of anti-Americanism, made him an unpromising if not inappropriate partner in a complex political process. We concluded that the prince's standing as a nationalist and the political legitimacy that he would bring to a settlement were valuable assets that might facilitate reconciliation in an otherwise polarized Khmer political environment. The challenge was to use Sihanouk's standing among the Khmer without having him dominate the process of constructing a political settlement. A consensus might never come to closure as he maneuvered—without a political organization or military forces—to establish himself as the balancer among the contending Khmer factions. We believed the UN Security Council could provide the structure and create the process that would contain the prince's maneuverings.

There was, however, an alternative approach—one advocated primarily by the Vietnamese and the Hun Sen regime—that asserted that such a UN role was a fundamental violation of Cambodia's sovereignty. They argued that preserving the integrity of the government and military capabilities of the State of Cambodia was the only way to prevent the Khmer Rouge from fighting or politicking their way back to power. This perspective, or elements of it, found some international support, and it had a number of passionate proponents in the United States.

Our critique of this perspective was based on the judgment that to build a settlement around Hun Sen would only further polarize Cambodia's politics and sustain the fighting. It would fail to draw on Prince Sihanouk's symbolic authority as the one Khmer leader with true legitimacy and national standing.[20] It would play to the political and military strengths of the Khmer Rouge at a time when no other force—no Khmer faction, country, or international organization—was interested in or capable of mounting effective military operations against them. China and Thailand, we assumed, would not tolerate consolidation of a Vietnamese surrogate regime in Phnom Penh. They would continue to give political support and armaments to the Khmer Rouge. The fighting would continue, magnifying the strengths of Pol Pot's troops as seasoned guerrilla fighters.

The best alternative, we believed, was to create a relatively neutral, internationally supervised political environment in Phnom Penh and to tolerate the Khmer Rouge's inclusion *in a limited and controlled way* in a UN-managed settlement process. This approach would control the hated Pol Pot regime through a UN peacekeeping presence and subject the regime's political legitimacy to the test of Cambodian public opinion.

---

20. We had every reason to believe that Sihanouk could not be induced to switch sides and ally himself with Hun Sen. The prince was too dependent on Chinese support; and he would compromise his position as a Khmer nationalist if he allied himself with a leader seen as a Vietnamese surrogate. And there were complex psychological issues of the royal Sihanouk making himself dependent on the power of a political-military leader of peasant background.

We could not imagine that the Khmer Rouge would prevail in a reasonably fair political contest; and by drawing on the authority and resources of the United Nations, we would enable—or pressure—China and Thailand to end their support of the Khmer Rouge.

Although this policy was hardly risk free as a way of constraining and undermining the Pol Pot regime, it seemed to the Bush administration a far better bet than backing Hun Sen in what would be an ongoing military conflict with the Khmer Rouge that seemed certain to have continuing Chinese and Thai support.

These contrasting perspectives shaped the politics—both international and domestic—of the Cambodia peace process for the next two years.[21]

In October 1989, I met in New York with Thai officials in order to assess the state of their efforts to broker a cease-fire among the Khmer factions. In late November I traveled to Australia and was informed by its foreign minister, Senator Gareth Evans, on November 23 that he was about to announce in the Australian Senate a major initiative on Cambodia also centered in the United Nations. And at the turn of the year, Secretary Baker sent letters of invitation to all his counterparts on the Security Council urging them to join in an effort to see whether the five permanent members could agree on the outlines of a settlement plan.

As events unfolded in 1990, reaching agreement among the Perm Five was easy relative to the complex processes of maintaining support from other interested international parties—especially the Thai, Japanese, and Australians—and, above all, developing domestic political backing for a UN-centered initiative.

---

21. Congressman Stephen J. Solarz laid out these policy perspectives in a lucid *Foreign Affairs* article. See Solarz, "Cambodia and the International Community," *Foreign Affairs* (spring 1990): esp. 109–110. As is detailed later, Solarz's advocacy in Congress for the Bush administration's Cambodia policy, which had been substantially influenced by his prior actions on the issue, became an essential element in building domestic political support for the administration's diplomacy.

Building a Security Council Consensus

The first of six Perm Five meetings convened in Paris on January 16–17, 1990, at the Hôtel de Crillon, a short distance from the U.S. embassy on Place de la Concorde.[22] After several hours of reviewing the results of the previous summer's Paris Conference, the U.S. delegation retired to the embassy with British counterparts in an effort to draft a set of basic principles by which to structure the work of the five.

To our surprise, the second day's plenary discussion revealed unanimous support for sixteen propositions we had drafted the previous evening.[23] The unchallenged addition of one more point proposed by the Russians— that the Perm Five would support responsible efforts by regional parties to achieve a comprehensive settlement—capped the list. The meeting established the agenda for what became the work of the next seven months. Beginning with the proposition that a military outcome was unacceptable, the Perm Five agreed that a political settlement required an "enhanced United Nations role." The document reaffirmed that the settlement had to be comprehensive; that the withdrawal of Vietnam's military forces from Cambodia had to be subject to verification by the United Nations; that the Khmer refugees in Thailand should return home in conditions of security; that the human rights of the population—an oblique reference to the violent practices of the Khmer Rouge—should be protected; and that the United Nations should manage a "free and fair" electoral process that would produce a new government. Recognizing that such a UN-managed settlement was a substantial intrusion into Cambodia's sovereignty, the five—drawing on the work of the Paris Conference—envisaged the formation of an ill-defined political body tentatively called a Supreme National Council (SNC) to be the "repository" of Cambodia's sovereignty during the transition to a new, popularly elected government.

Publication of the outline elicited relief in many quarters. It was not clear following suspension of the Paris Conference that there was any life left

---

22. The second meeting was in New York on February 11–13; the third in Paris on March 12–13; the fourth in New York on May 25–26; the fifth in Paris on July 16–17; and the final session in New York on August 27–28.

23. See "Text of the UN Declaration on the Conflict in Cambodia," *New York Times*, January 17, 1990.

in the international effort to bring peace to Cambodia. Yet the January document did little more than identify the central issues that had to be explored in detail if an operational plan for a settlement was to be created. How would security in the country be maintained if the Khmer political factions continued to test their strength on the battlefield? Would UN personnel even enter the country in the absence of a cease-fire among the factional armies, and what would happen to those armies? How to repatriate the hundreds of thousands of Khmer refugees who had been encamped in Thailand on Cambodia's western border for more than a decade? How to protect the human rights of a population that for more than a decade had been ravaged by genocidal violence, social revolution, and warfare? Who would run the government pending elections? And who would pay the substantial costs of a settlement? To advance consideration of these issues, the Perm Five scheduled a second round of consultations in New York on February 11.

The second session was shaped by three intersecting layers of military action, politics, and diplomacy. In Cambodia, the resistance forces of Sihanouk, Son Sann, and the Khmer Rouge were gaining some ground from Hun Sen's troops, putting significant pressure on Hun Sen and the Vietnamese for a settlement that would weaken outside support for the resistance coalition. Despite the military action, the prospect of a political settlement involving the United Nations seemed sufficiently within reach that Secretary-General Javier Pérez de Cuéllar and his special representative for Cambodia, Rafeeuddin Ahmed, briefed the U.S. delegation prior to the second Perm Five meeting. Ahmed reviewed the full range of issues that would have to be addressed if the United Nations was to manage a settlement process. Perm Five discussion of the terms of a settlement, in turn, was shaped by persisting differences between China (representing the Khmer Rouge as well as its own interests) on the one hand and the Soviet Union (speaking for the Vietnamese and Hun Sen) on the other hand.

The February meeting, and those of March, May, and July, elaborated on three core aspects of a settlement: how to end the fighting and control the factions' military units; how to account for Cambodia's sovereignty during the transition to election of a new government; and how to administer the country. The five readily agreed that to stabilize a cease-fire, the contending military forces should be put under UN control in cantonments where they would be disarmed and eventually reorganized into a new national army under the authority of the Cambodian government that would emerge from the elections. (Getting the Khmer factions to agree to this process, or some variant of it, however, became the focus of another year of diplomacy and political maneuvering.)

The issue of how to constitute the Supreme National Council was burdened with the highly contentious matter of whether to include the feared Khmer Rouge in a settlement process at all. To give them some formal standing would imply a measure of legitimacy and an opportunity to regain power through UN-managed elections. The Chinese made clear that they would not support a UN settlement from which the Khmer Rouge were fully excluded. For the Bush administration this was the central political issue: including the Khmer Rouge in any form might well undermine congressional support for a UN—or any other—settlement plan. The dilemma was ultimately resolved at the July session when the Perm Five agreed that the Supreme National Council should be composed of "*individuals* representing the full range of Cambodian public opinion" (italics mine) and deprived of any operational authority.

By thus eliding the membership issue, and by creating a mechanism of only symbolic weight, we avoided recognizing the Khmer Rouge *as an organization*, even though their foreign minister, Khieu Samphan, as an individual would represent the forces of Pol Pot. He would become one of the guardians of Cambodia's sovereign rights. This arrangement, we estimated, gave the Chinese sufficient political leverage to "deliver" their hated client to the settlement. Yet we believed it would so constrain the Khmer Rouge within the UN-managed process that their chances of regaining power by political means were minimized.

The question of how to administer the country during the transition to elections reflected the same issues of sovereignty and political control that burdened discussion of the Supreme National Council. The problem was how to deal with the existing governmental structure of Hun Sen's State of Cambodia. At the March meeting the Perm Five agreed that the United Nations should form a "transitional authority" as the vehicle for international supervision of the settlement process, but the scope of this authority was a matter of substantial contention. The Chinese initially pressed for complete dismantling of Hun Sen's government, while the Russians called for a minimal UN oversight role in both the transitional administration and the election process. By July, however, the Chinese showed enough flexibility to enable the Perm Five to agree that UNTAC should be mandated to assume "supervision or control of the existing administrative structures."

At the February meeting the UN secretary-general established a special task force to begin planning for UNTAC operations, which were to be led by his then–under secretary for public information, Yasushi Akashi. With Perm Five blessing, several UN planning missions were sent to Cambodia in the spring and summer to evaluate the requirements of controlling Hun Sen's administrative structure and repatriating the refugees on the Thai border. The missions also assessed such security issues as demining the countryside and controlling the military forces of the four factions.

The U.S. and British delegations pressed the issue of protecting the human rights of the Khmer people as a way of dealing with the threat of Pol Pot's return. The Soviets, mirroring Thach's use of the "genocide" issue, initially pressed for explicit reference to the need for measures to control Pol Pot. By the March meeting, however, they dropped their use of the term "genocide"—which would invariably elicit a counter from the Chinese—and agreed to the indirect formulation developed at the Paris Conference of the need to "undertake effective measures to ensure that the policies and practices of the past shall never be allowed to return." These included agreement at the May meeting that the United Nations should formally monitor and protect the human rights of the Cambodian people as an integral part of the settlement.

Controlling the factional military forces was the most contentious of the settlement issues. It was not resolved until the eve of final agreement on the peace plan in August 1991. The initial Perm Five discussions were divided along predictable lines, with the Soviets supporting the Vietnamese in their determination that Hun Sen's forces remain intact. Only gradually did agreement develop on a program of ending foreign military assistance to the factional armies, placing them in cantonments and disarming and retraining the troops. There was no agreement on the size of a UN peacekeeping force, and whether it should only monitor the departure of the Vietnamese forces and supervise the return of the refugees or take on the much more complex and dangerous tasks of disarming and reorganizing the factions. (Ultimately, the United Nations deployed in Cambodia an international peacekeeping contingent of 16,000, supported by 5,000 civilian administrative personnel, for a period of eighteen months.)

It was at this point of substantial progress in the Perm Five discussions that Secretary Baker made his third critical intervention affecting the dynamic of the mediation effort. During the fall of 1989 and into the spring of 1990, domestic political pressure in the United States had been building against *any* agreement that would seem to legitimate the Khmer Rouge by including their leadership in a settlement plan, much less increase the party's chance of returning to power by some combination of military and political maneuvering. I faced unrelenting criticism on this issue in congressional hearings. And certain American mass media figures were trying to make the case that the Bush administration's activities in Cambodia were strengthening, indirectly if not directly, covertly if not openly, Pol Pot's military forces.

In early July a bipartisan group of sixty-six senators led by Democrat George Mitchell of Maine and Republican John Danforth of Missouri sent Secretary Baker a letter urging the administration to withdraw its support for the Sihanouk–Khmer Rouge political coalition, the CGDK, still occupying Cambodia's seat at the United Nations. The letter debunked the notion that a political settlement would lead to China withdrawing its support for the Khmer Rouge ("China is the problem, not the solution in Cambodia") and that U.S. policy "should be based, first and foremost, upon preventing the return to power of the Khmer Rouge." Although they did not explicitly call for a settlement based on support for Hun Sen's State of Cambodia, the senators asserted that it was "counterproductive for the United States to decline all contact with the Hun Sen regime." They called for easing restrictions on humanitarian and development aid for (Hun Sen's) Cambodia. The implicit warning behind this letter was that if the administration did not shift its approach to a Cambodian settlement away from Sihanouk's coalition, Congress would cut off all financial support for the noncommunist resistance—FUNCINPEC and the KPNLF.[24]

The sum of these pressures impelled an adjustment in our Cambodia policy. The alternative was to have Congress impose a set of restrictions or conditions that would tie the administration's hands as a negotiating party and likely produce a collapse of the delicately balanced house of cards that we were constructing through the Perm Five consultations. We were in a race between the growth of domestic political forces determined to oppose any deal involving the Khmer Rouge, no matter what the alternative, and the conclusion of a Perm Five–Security Council consensus on a UN-centered process. In a manner not anticipated at the time, the secretary of state took an initiative that helped precipitate a successful end game of the Perm Five consultations.

On July 18, 1990, as we were concluding the fifth Perm Five session in Paris, Secretary Baker was meeting in the same city with his Soviet counterpart, Foreign Minister Eduard Shevardnadze. Emerging from the ministerial discussion, the secretary announced to the press that the United States was withdrawing its support for the CGDK, Sihanouk's diplomatic coalition with the Khmer Rouge, as the legitimate incumbent in Cambodia's UN seat. Baker added that, in the search for peace in

---

24. This situation was a reprise of the congressional cutoff of support for the Lon Nol government in 1973, an action that in some measure accelerated the Khmer Rouge's coming to power. See Kissinger, *Years of Upheaval,* 349–369, and *Years of Renewal,* 496–519.

Cambodia, the United States would initiate consultations with the Vietnamese government and was even considering contacts with Hun Sen.

I had presaged this development with the Chinese a few days earlier by showing them the letter from the sixty-six senators to the secretary as evidence of the intense domestic political pressures on our policy. Secretary Baker had informed Shevardnadze of the shift in our position just minutes before meeting with the press. In its effect, this tactical move was a political bombshell for all those involved in the negotiations. It implied that the United States had switched sides and was now tilting toward Vietnam in the search for peace in Cambodia, and that the administration was closely coordinating policy with the Soviet Union.

The Chinese responded to the secretary's announcement by publicly expressing strong "disappointment" with the development. Privately they told us that the shift had caused "confusion" in their leadership about our policies. (Yet behind the scenes, and largely unknown to us at the time, Beijing was in the process of shifting its own policy toward Vietnam.) The concern of the Chinese, as with the even sharper public criticism of the move by Indonesian foreign minister Alatas, was that this U.S. opening toward Hanoi would stiffen the resistance of the Vietnamese and Hun Sen to the nearly completed UN settlement plan, and perhaps encourage other countries to work for a settlement outside the Perm Five framework.[25]

In fact, the secretary's move put China under heightened pressure to come to closure in the Perm Five consultations as a way of keeping the Khmer Rouge on the track of a political—as opposed to a military—settlement. And we gave the Vietnamese, increasingly isolated as the communist world began to collapse in Eastern Europe and then the Soviet Union, an opening

---

25. The "Baker shift," as it was called by the Japanese, did encourage Tokyo to press ahead with its initiative, together with the Thai, for a Hun Sen–Sihanouk coalition as the core of a political settlement. See Masaharu Kohno, *In Search of Proactive Diplomacy,* esp. 27–28.

to improve relations with the United States. We did so by reiterating in bilateral contacts the linkage between their support for a UN-managed settlement in Cambodia and normalization of U.S.-Vietnam relations.[26]

The sixth Perm Five session convened in New York five weeks after the Baker announcement, and the final elements of a settlement framework quickly fell into place. The United Nations, through UNTAC, would take control of Cambodia's key governmental functions during a transition to elections. The refugees on Thailand's border with Cambodia would be repatriated under UN supervision, and the United Nations would verify the departure of all Vietnamese forces from the country. Cambodia's sovereignty would be "embodied" in a Supreme National Council composed of individuals, not organizations, and the body would have no operational authority pending UN supervised elections. The Khmer military forces would be placed in cantonments and disarmed pending their reorganization into a new national army. And the international community would take measures through the United Nations to safeguard the human rights of the Cambodian people.

On August 28 the five permanent members of the Security Council publicly announced their agreement on this framework for a UN-centered, comprehensive political settlement of the Cambodia conflict.

---

26. The Reagan administration had maintained low-key contacts with the Vietnamese in the interest of resolving POW/MIA issues. These contacts stressed the need for Vietnam to withdraw from Cambodia, as well as to resolve several hundred "last known alive discrepancy cases," as a basis for normalizing relations. See Richard T. Childress and Stephen J. Solarz, "Vietnam: Detours on the Road to Normalization," in *Reversing Relations with Former Adversaries: U.S. Foreign Policy after the Cold War*, ed. C. Richard Nelson and Kenneth Weisbrode (Gainesville: University of Florida Press, 1998). The Bush administration held its first formal bilateral consultation with the Vietnamese in New York on August 6, 1990, three weeks after the Baker announcement. Deputy Assistant Secretary of State Kenneth Quinn represented the United States; Vietnam's permanent representative to the United Nations, Trinh Xuan Lang, represented Hanoi. The subjects of discussion were the Cambodia peace process and the requirements for improving U.S.-Vietnam relations.

Reaching this point in the peace process reflected the significant degree of international consensus on the elements of a settlement that had emerged over a decade of diplomacy, especially through the JIM and Paris Conference efforts. The progress was, as well, an expression of the degree to which great power relations were changing as the Cold War approached its end. Yet getting this far had required complex, multilay-ered diplomacy that affected the interests of a number of states that were not permanent members of the Security Council, and further progress would continue to do so. Following through on the Perm Five frame-work agreement took more than an additional year of intense diplomacy to bring the four Khmer factions to accept it. And concurrent with the UN-centered effort, other interested countries were exploring alterna-tive paths to a settlement.

Herding Cats

The Bush administration's early approach to the diplomacy of a Cambodian settlement had been to let ASEAN and France take the lead. With success in building the Perm Five framework agreement, however, we acquired a certain measure of paternity and vested interest in the semiformed UN settlement plan. In the early fall of 1990 we began an effort that took nearly a year to broaden support for the framework agreement within the international community, and to encourage the countries backing the various Khmer factions to gain the cooperation of their surrogates for the UN-centered process. This proved to be a challenging but not impossible task. The Perm Five effort had acquired a momentum and authority that proved difficult for governments with other ideas and other interests either to resist or to subvert. My instructions from Under Secretary of State Robert Kimmit were to work along with these other initiatives, which came from allies in the Asian region, but also to protect our investment in the advancing Security Council effort.

One alternative approach was promoted by the government of Chatichai Choonhavan in Thailand. Prime Minister Chatichai had been voted into office in mid-1988 to form the first civilian Thai government in a decade. Early in his tenure he had promoted a policy of transforming Indochina "from a battlefield into a marketplace." In this effort he had the support of two trusted civilian special advisers, his son, Kraisak Choonhavan, and Kraisak's colleague Pansak Vinyaratin. The two were an irrepressible duo who came to be dubbed, with some affection, the "Bobsy twins" of Cambodia diplomacy. They were concerned about Thai passivity in dealing with the unresolved conflict on their country's eastern frontier, a matter of immediate concern to Thailand's national security and economic interests. With the apparent failure of the Paris Conference effort in the summer of 1989, they embarked with enthusiasm on a diplomatic effort to form a Cambodian government based on a Hun Sen–Sihanouk coalition.

In late April 1989 the Thai government had hosted a "seminar" of senior officials from all the Indochina states to build support for the prime minister's vision of transforming all of Southeast Asia into a "Golden

Peninsula" of economic growth.[27] Chatichai's conception, however enticing, was to succumb to four fatal flaws: it implicitly pitted capitalist Thailand allied to the United States against socialist Vietnam allied to the Soviet Union, and the Vietnamese were not (yet) prepared to cede leadership in the region to a longtime strategic and ideological rival; it would require Sihanouk to abandon his CGDK allies and side with Hun Sen; and Thailand would have to break with the ASEAN consensus on Cambodia policy. It also required domestic political support, when in fact the policy was splitting the Chatichai administration from the Thai military, which was determined to resist Vietnamese influence in Cambodia through support for the Khmer Rouge, and from the Foreign Ministry, which was committed to sustaining close relations with ASEAN and the United States.

After suspension of the Paris Conference, however, Chatichai saw in the impasse an opening for a diplomatic initiative. On September 11 he announced that he would try to broker a cease-fire among the Khmer factions before the Vietnamese withdrew their troops at the end of the month.[28] His effort required some shuttle diplomacy. He and his advisers moved among the factions and then traveled to Beijing to make a direct appeal to the Chinese for support for their plan. China's backing was a prerequisite for getting Sihanouk to end his coalition with the Khmer Rouge. This effort fizzled when the factions resisted a cease-fire. The Khmer Rouge took a major battlefield initiative in late October that led to their capture of the gem-mining town of Pailin, only a few miles from Thailand's eastern border with Cambodia.[29]

---

27. See Steven Erlanger, "Thailand Seeks to Shape a 'Golden Peninsula,'" *New York Times,* April 30, 1989.

28. Steven Erlanger, "Thai Leader Trying to Break Cambodian Impasse," *New York Times,* September 11, 1989.

29. See Rodney Tasker, "Another Year Zero?" *Far Eastern Economic Review,* November 9, 1989.

Chatichai's advisers were not deterred by this setback. In the spring of 1990 they responded to an appeal from the director of the First Southeast Asia Division of the Japanese Foreign Ministry, Masaharu Kohno, to join forces in a further effort to entice Prince Sihanouk into a coalition with Hun Sen.[30] Their appeal was strengthened with the prospect of Japanese economic support for Cambodia's reconstruction. They also calculated, with some justification, that the growing success of the Khmer Rouge on the battlefield might now interest Sihanouk in "tilting" toward Hun Sen so as to give greater balance to his position. As well, the Thai advisers (and we ourselves) were not sure at this point that the Perm Five consultations, still in midcourse, would succeed in reaching a consensus. They pressed ahead for a "regional" settlement built around Sihanouk and Hun Sen.

The advisers wanted to gain U.S. support for their initiative, and hence proposed that I meet secretly with them to coordinate policy before a Hun Sen–Sihanouk summit conference they were planning with the Japanese for early June.[31] Their objective was to gain American support for their regional approach; mine was to convince them of the value of the Perm Five process and to keep lines open to two allied governments. The Bush administration's risk in agreeing to the "secret" meeting, in the ever-conspiratorial world of Asian politics, was that as word of the encounter leaked out (which we assumed it would) we would sow distrust or confusion among our ASEAN colleagues or even weaken the growing Perm Five consensus. Despite these liabilities, I traveled unannounced to Rome in late May for a day of talks with Pansak Vinyaratin. We each made our case, and on June 4 Prince Sihanouk met with Hun Sen in Tokyo at the Japanese-hosted summit.

The Japanese-Thai effort initially seemed to succeed, for the Tokyo summit ended with the announcement of a cease-fire among the factions and an agreement between the two delegations (Sihanouk and Hun Sen)

---

30. See Masaharu Kohno, *In Search of Proactive Diplomacy*, 28–29.

31. Nayan Chanda, "Japan's Quiet Entrance on the Diplomatic Stage," *Christian Science Monitor*, June 13, 1990.

to join a reconvened Paris Conference that would conclude a settlement on a "two governments" basis. Yet key issues remained unresolved. Kraisak Choonhavan came to Washington with his father in mid-June, shortly after the Tokyo summit, for a meeting with President Bush. Kraisak informed me that Hun Sen had not accepted an "enhanced role" for the United Nations in a settlement. He also said that Sihanouk had left Tokyo uncertain about how he would deal with the Khmer Rouge. They had boycotted the Tokyo session because of their opposition to the "two governments" negotiation that the French, Thai, and Japanese were planning for Paris. "Let Sihanouk figure out how to deal with the KR [Khmer Rouge]," Kraisak told me dismissively.

During his Washington visit, Prime Minister Chatichai informed President Bush that he foresaw the cease-fire leading to elections monitored by some (unspecified) form of international control mechanism and the formation of a coalition government organized in the Thai model of a constitutional monarchy. Under such an arrangement Sihanouk would be largely a symbolic figure, with political and administrative power in the hands of a prime minister—Hun Sen. Chatichai expressed confidence that China would gain Khmer Rouge support for such an arrangement.

Within two months, however, the Japanese-Thai initiative collapsed. Following the Tokyo summit, Sihanouk returned to his residence in Beijing and apparently encountered intense pressure from the Khmer Rouge and the Chinese to repudiate the Tokyo agreement. He did so publicly on September 4, just a week after publication of the Perm Five framework agreement, calling instead for an interim administration of Cambodia structured with equal representation from all four Khmer factions.

At the turn of the year Chatichai's government was deposed by the Thai military on charges of corruption. The activist advisers, Kraisak and Pansak, were now out of the Cambodia negotiations; the successor military government in Bangkok reaffirmed Thailand's support for the ASEAN consensus on Cambodia and the now-advancing UN settlement process.

So, too, did the Japanese, although the Foreign Ministry continued to chafe at Japan's peripheral role in the negotiations. Masaharu Kohno confided to me, "We don't want to just sit and watch the outcome [of the diplomacy] idly in the stadium and then do the cleanup after the game is over [that is, pay for Cambodia's reconstruction]."[32] The reason behind Japan's second-rank status in the diplomacy was not U.S. resistance to its playing an active role, but the fact that Japan was not a permanent member of the UN Security Council. We made assiduous efforts to brief our Japanese counterparts, as well as those from ASEAN and Australia, before and after each Perm Five session. The Japanese would send special delegations to Paris or New York for direct and immediate readouts. But this consultative approach was insufficient for governments with serious interests in the outcome of the negotiations, especially those facing considerable domestic political pressure to be significant players in shaping the terms of a settlement.

The need to play a significant role applied as much as anyone to the Australians. The Hawke government, with its articulate foreign minister, Senator Gareth Evans, in the lead, was trying to shape Australia's Asian environment in anticipation of the end of the Cold War. And like the Bush administration, the Hawke government was under considerable pressure from Parliament to formulate a Cambodia settlement in such a way that the Khmer Rouge would be blocked from regaining power. The Australians play their politics much like they play rugby, with rough-and-tumble scrums and a good deal of open-field running. This was the character of our relationship with the government in Canberra as the Cambodia negotiations advanced.[33]

---

32. See Masaharu Kohno, *In Search of Proactive Diplomacy*, 25, footnote 28.

33. In 1989–92 the government in Canberra took a number of diplomatic initiatives involving U.S. interests, initially without prior consultation. In 1989 the Australians joined with the Japanese to launch a regional economic cooperation organization that eventually became the Asia-Pacific Economic Cooperation (APEC) forum. In its first articulation, APEC did not include the United States, a curious omission given the importance of economic relations with the United States to both countries. See Keith

In the fall of 1989, as we were laying the groundwork for the secretary of state to launch the Perm Five effort, Foreign Minister Evans's ministry was preparing what came to be called "the Red Book." The volume, which pulled together much of the discussion at the Paris Conference, was a compendium of issues and possible solutions that had to be dealt with in constructing a UN-administered settlement of the Cambodian conflict.[34] In early December Evans dispatched his deputy, Michael Costello, on a tour of Asia to gain support for what was termed "Australia's United Nations peace plan."[35] Costello visited China and the relevant countries in Southeast Asia and met with the Khmer factions, including the Khmer Rouge. This effort proceeded in parallel with the beginnings of the Perm Five consultations in Paris and New York. Following publication of the first and second Perm Five joint communiqués, which expressed support for an "enhanced UN role" in a settlement, the Evans's initiative merged with ASEAN's Cambodia diplomacy, leading to a new JIM meeting in Jakarta at the end of February 1990.

Foreign Ministers Alatas of Indonesia and Evans of Australia succeeded in getting the four Khmer factions together, along with Vietnam's Thach and representatives of other regional states, in an effort to build support for the "enhanced UN" approach. The Khmer verbally agreed to have the

---

Scott, *Gareth Evans* (St. Leonards, Australia: Allen and Unwin, 1999), 271–272. The Evans Cambodia initiative, premised on a lead UN role in the settlement, was launched with little prior consultation with either the United Nations or members of the Security Council. And in 1992 Evans floated the idea of a Conference on Security and Cooperation in Asia (CSCA), in parallel with a similarly named organization in Europe. Again, the initiative was taken without prior consultation with the United States, another curiously independent approach given the relevance of the U.S. military presence in East Asia to Australia's security interests. Domestic political forces impel many governments to demonstrate that they are "out in front" and doing the right thing on issues important to the nation's interests, even at the expense of prior consultations with allies and other potential supporters.

34. See Gareth Evans, *Cooperating for Peace: The Global Agenda for the 1990s and Beyond* (St. Leonards, Australia: Allen and Unwin, 1993), 107–108.

35. See Gareth Evans and Bruce Grant, *Australia's Foreign Relations in the World of the 1990s* (Melbourne: Melbourne University Press, 1991, 1995), 210–218.

United Nations deploy a peacekeeping force and administer elections, but the meeting collapsed when Thach raised the same issue of "genocide" that had deadlocked the Paris Conference. Thach and Hun Sen also opposed the establishment of a Supreme National Council headed by Prince Sihanouk as the governing authority in the transition to elections, stressing instead the need to maintain administration by Hun Sen's State of Cambodia.[36] The two continued to block progress toward a consensus among the Khmer factions for more than a year, even as Thach tried to cultivate a positive relationship with the United States.

The Australian initiative, though initially unsuccessful, played an important role in mobilizing international support for a UN-managed settlement and in linking the results of the Paris Conference to the diplomacy of defining an operational plan for peace in Cambodia. As the Perm Five consensus on a framework agreement grew, Evans's effort naturally merged with it.

Behind Canberra's support for the UN-centered process, however, domestic Australian political tensions persisted over the issue of the role of the Khmer Rouge in a settlement. This was the same issue that was polarizing U.S. domestic politics: a UN transitional authority for the Cambodian settlement that included an essentially powerless Supreme National Council involving individuals representing the Khmer Rouge versus the alternative of a settlement built around Hun Sen and his State of Cambodia.

Prior to initiation of the Perm Five process, Australia's ambassador to Bangkok, Richard Butler, had publicly attacked the Paris-ASEAN notion of a comprehensive settlement. Instead, Butler supported the position of Chatichai and his advisers that a more limited settlement should be constructed around Hun Sen. Butler was criticized by his own government

---

36. See Hamish McDonald, "Entrenched Positions," *Far Eastern Economic Review,* March 15, 1990, 13.

for publicly challenging the ASEAN position, but other pro–Hun Sen forces in Australia continued to press for a settlement that would exclude the Khmer Rouge and preserve the integrity of the State of Cambodia.[37]

These tensions were evident in U.S.-Australian relations in the spring of 1990 as the Perm Five pressed ahead with the design of a Supreme National Council that would somehow involve the Khmer Rouge. One night I received a call at home from Evans's deputy, Michael Costello, to review our respective positions in the evolving UN settlement mechanism. I was startled when Costello warned me not to support an SNC that would include the Khmer Rouge and weaken the State of Cambodia. "We'll remember who brought back the Khmer Rouge," he threatened, "and one day there will be an accounting."

Costello's threat reflected the deepening political controversy around the evolving UN settlement plan. We felt the tension most immediately in our day-to-day efforts to build support in the United States for the Perm Five plan.

---

37. Tasker, "Another Year Zero?" 12–13.

Domestic Political Fury

One of the distinguishing characteristics of U.S. foreign policy in the twentieth century has been the divide between the imperatives of realpolitik or balance of power politics on the one hand, and moral or human rights concerns on the other hand.[38] Since World War II and the Nazi holocaust, no issue has embodied these tensions more than that of mass political violence. The United States, in practice, has at best a sluggish record in responding to situations of mass political murder—as most recently in Rwanda and Bosnia—or in supporting the development of a permanent and robust international legal regime to cope with the aftermath of gross violations of human rights. Nonetheless, genocide is a powerful symbol in our domestic foreign policy debates. This was certainly the case in the politics of a Cambodia settlement, where public concern with the Khmer Rouge's systematic murder of between 1 to 2 million Cambodians between 1975 and 1978 dominated the U.S. public's attitude toward the settlement process.

The human rights aspect of the Cambodia negotiations gained heightened political force when the Chinese government, in early June 1989, violently suppressed peaceful demonstrators at Tiananmen, just as we were preparing for the Paris Conference. The Bush administration was headed by a president who had developed close relations with the Chinese during his days as chief of the U.S. Liaison Office in Beijing. Given his lead role in dealings with China, the president came under sharp and persistent domestic political attacks for what were characterized as insufficient efforts to censure the Chinese for the violence at Tiananmen, for seeking to maintain the U.S.-China relationship, for "coddling dictators." During the Cambodia negotiations, the administration was criticized for supporting China's effort to counter Vietnamese influence in Indochina, at the presumed cost of ignoring the Khmer Rouge threat. This public attack had potency in the context of our domestic political cycle, given the approaching 1990 midterm elections and, two years further down the road, the 1992 presidential contest.

---

38. See Henry A. Kissinger, *Diplomacy* (New York: Simon and Schuster, 1994), esp. chapter 2.

When the Vietnamese withdrew their forces from Cambodia in 1988 and 1989, informed American observers urged the Bush administration to pressure the Chinese to cut off arms shipments to the Khmer Rouge— something we had been doing repeatedly, but to no evident effect, in diplomatic channels[39]—and to prevent their inclusion in any governing authority in Cambodia.[40] A few public figures went so far as to say that the Khmer Rouge danger was so great that the United States should break with Sihanouk and support Hun Sen, or at least press for a Hun Sen–Sihanouk coalition. Hun Sen's government, asserted a former director of the CIA, "is clearly preferable … to another Khmer Rouge government."[41]

This was an appealing position that might well have gained the administration's support after the Vietnamese withdrew their forces from Cambodia, but as a political strategy it was based on a flawed assessment of the dynamics of the Cambodian situation: Sihanouk was dependent on Chinese support; and the Chinese would not back away from the Khmer Rouge as long as they saw Vietnam as a stalking-horse for Moscow's effort to encircle them, or as long as the Vietnamese were determined to preserve their influence in Cambodia. Hence we concluded that it was fruitless to press Sihanouk to break with his Khmer coalition partners and the Chinese in the absence of a comprehensive settlement.[42] For the

---

39. Although the Carter administration tolerated, if not encouraged, Chinese support for the Khmer Rouge as a source of pressure on the Vietnamese after their invasion of Cambodia, Secretary of State George Shultz, during the Reagan administration, began urging the Chinese to switch their support to the noncommunist resistance, a position that was maintained in the Bush administration.

40. See, for example, Frederick Z. Brown and Paul H. Kreisberg, "Speaking Out against the Khmer Rouge," *Christian Science Monitor,* June 2, 1988.

41. Jeremy J. Stone and William E. Colby, "Block the Khmer Rouge," *New York Times,* April 28, 1989. For a detailed retrospective account of a "pro–Hun Sen" position, see Jeremy J. Stone, *"Every Man Should Try": Adventures of a Public Interest Activist* (New York: Perseus Books, Public Affairs, 1999), 257–291.

42. We also had reason to believe that the Chinese were interested in a political settlement in Cambodia that would stabilize the country and enable China to back away from the Khmer Rouge. Deng Xiaoping met with Secretary of State George Shultz in July 1988 and raised the issue of Cambodia in a way that suggested he was defining China's terms for a negotiated resolution of the conflict.

United States to side with the Hun Sen government on its own would only have polarized Cambodian politics in circumstances in which the United States was unprepared to involve itself in an open-ended guerrilla war against the Khmer Rouge. But the moral imperative of opposing genocidal murderers trapped the administration in an unsustainable political position at home: so long as we supported Sihanouk, we seemed to be supporting—or at least not actively opposing—the Khmer Rouge.

This moral and political dilemma was dramatically exposed during my first congressional testimony on Cambodia policy on September 14, 1989, a little more than two weeks after suspension of the Paris Conference. In three hours of intense and emotional review of the outcome of the conference, representatives from both sides of the political aisle roundly criticized the Bush administration for going along with the Sihanouk-ASEAN position that the transitional authority in Cambodia should be a quadripartite governing body including the Khmer Rouge.

Our counterargument—that our allies in the region advocated inclusion of the Khmer Rouge as the best way to move the conflict from the battlefield to the ballot box—gained few supporters. Republican congressman Jim Leach of Iowa, noting that by our own admission the administration had not taken the lead at Paris, urged that we take the moral high ground and distance the United States as far as possible from the Khmer Rouge and their Chinese supporters. Democratic congressman Chester Atkins from Massachusetts' Fifth Congressional District, which contained a sizable Khmer community, said he was "angry as hell" because the U.S. delegation, according to his information, had remained silent on the issue of preventing genocide (which was not the case). Atkins implied that the administration should withdraw its support from Sihanouk and the noncommunist resistance and "take a fresh and more reasoned assessment of the successes of the Hun Sen government."[43]

---

43. All quotations and summary assessments of congressional testimony cited in this study are drawn from the *Congressional Record* or records of the relevant committee hearings of the relevant dates.

To accommodate this criticism, of course, would have required accepting the Vietnamese–Hun Sen position put forward at Paris. To do so would have meant abandoning a political process designed to break China's military support for the Khmer Rouge, controlling them with a UN peacekeeping force and creating a new Cambodian government through internationally supervised elections.

Fortunately, the alternative of a UN-managed settlement, which we were in the process of designing, was a way to break out of this political trap. More to the point, it was the best way to deal with the real-world threat of the Khmer Rouge. The contentious congressional hearing in early September gave us every incentive to abandon our relatively passive diplomatic posture and take the initiative in shaping the terms of a peace process. Neither Congress nor the administration had any interest in a *unilateral* American effort to bring peace to Cambodia, which very likely would have required deploying U.S. forces to control the Khmer Rouge. The United Nations, through the Security Council, seemed to provide the best alternative of a workable way to attain our policy objectives, as Secretary of State Baker had defined them on the way to the Paris Conference.

Our public debate, however, did not define the issue in these terms. Successive American administrations—under Presidents Carter, Reagan, and Bush—had encouraged the formation and growth of a noncommunist resistance as an alternative to a settlement that would be a choice between two communist factions, Pol Pot's "Democratic Kampuchea" versus Hun Sen's "State of Cambodia." This approach, however, was weakened by Prince Sihanouk's anti–Hun Sen *political* coalition with the Khmer Rouge.

The Provocative Role of the Media

n late April 1990 this situation was given national television prominence by ABC News, which aired a special program, "From the Killing Fields," hosted by anchorman Peter Jennings.[44] The program was constructed to expose the "fact" that American aid to Sihanouk was strengthening the Khmer Rouge, that there was a secret program of military assistance to the communists, and that the prince's forces and the Khmer Rouge were conducting joint military operations against Hun Sen's forces. Jennings attempted to make his case around a provocative statement by Sihanouk that implied the United States was supporting Pol Pot's fighters because they were the most effective means of countering Vietnam's occupation of Cambodia. Jennings also took out of context a statement of mine that obliquely implied that U.S. aid for the noncommunist Khmer—which was non-lethal in character—was getting to Pol Pot's forces, something that we had no evidence was occurring.[45]

Fortunately, Jennings's opening material in this special program was followed by an on-the-air discussion that included informed and credible observers of the Cambodian scene such as Congressman Stephen Solarz, former assistant secretary of state Richard Holbrooke, and our ambassador to the United Nations, Thomas Pickering. Both Solarz and Pickering debunked Jennings's premise. The panel discussion deflated the objective of the program. Yet the issue persisted in congressional attacks on

44. See Robert Koehler, "A Tougher Peter Jennings Probes Cambodia Quandary," *Los Angeles Times*, April 26, 1990.

45. During this period we received occasional intelligence reports of battlefield encounters between Khmer Rouge and noncommunist military units, and perhaps instances of coordinated actions, reflecting the fact that the three militaries were operating in a very restricted physical space. The units of the Sihanouk and Son Sann armies, however, were decidedly undersupplied relative to the Khmer Rouge, and field commanders may have on occasion sought materiel from communist units—not the other way around. As a matter of policy, however, both Prince Ranarridh and Son Sann rejected joint military operations with the Khmer Rouge, and they communicated this policy formally to both the United States and their own field commanders.

Sihanouk's political coalition with the Khmer Rouge and on the administration's policy of supporting Sihanouk.[46]

A year later, on April 10, 1991, the eve of one of my last presentations before Congress, ABC News broadcast another provocative Cambodia story. The Jennings nightly news program aired film purporting to show Sihanouk's forces conducting a joint military operation with the Khmer Rouge. Such evidence, if true, would be grounds for cutting off all American aid to Sihanouk and Son Sann. Fortunately, the evening broadcast was aired fifteen hours before my scheduled congressional testimony. Because of the time difference between Washington and Bangkok, we were able to confirm overnight from U.S. embassy sources that the filmed "evidence" was in fact a staged encounter between Sihanouk and Khmer Rouge units that ABC News had purchased from a freelance photographer operating out of Thailand. During my testimony the next day before the House Subcommittee on Asian and Pacific Affairs, I was able to undermine the credibility of the "evidence." The timing of the ABC broadcast, however, revealed the close coordination that had developed between congressional opponents of the administration's policy and at least one national news organization.

This same congressional session included one of the last attacks on a key premise of our policy, that the UN settlement plan, whatever its limitations, was the best vehicle for preventing the Khmer Rouge from regaining power. House Chairman Solarz took the unusual step of inviting Congressman Atkins to testify at the hearing. Atkins, in an impassioned prepared presentation, asserted that the UN peace process made the United States party to a settlement that would legitimate the Khmer Rouge and help them regain power. He denigrated Sihanouk for working with the Chinese and their unholy agent Pol Pot and urged an end to a policy of "isolating, punishing and condemning" the Hun Sen regime, which he asserted "has the only army protecting the Cambodian people from the

---

46. See, for example, my testimony before the Senate Foreign Relations Subcommittee on Asian and Pacific Affairs on July 20, 1990.

Khmer Rouge." He called for "the immediate cessation of all aid to the noncommunist resistance," urged that the UN plan should be modified to exclude Khmer Rouge participation in the Supreme National Council, and advocated U.S. humanitarian aid to Hun Sen's government and support for an international tribunal to bring to justice Pol Pot, Ieng Sary, Nuon Chea, Son Sen, Ta Mok, and the other top Khmer Rouge leaders.

Chairman Solarz's response to Atkins's critique was a withering cross-examination of his congressional colleague. His questioning made the case that the UN plan was the only credible alternative for pursuing the objective of preventing the Khmer Rouge from regaining power. Solarz observed that Atkins's assessment of circumstances in Cambodia was "fundamentally incompatible with the realities of the situation." He noted that the Perm Five had abandoned the Paris Conference concept of a quadripartite transitional governing body composed of all the Khmer factions in favor of a UN-administered transition, with Cambodia's sovereignty represented in the essentially powerless Supreme National Council. Solarz asserted that the UN peace process would in fact undermine the Khmer Rouge by cutting off their support from China and Thailand, control them within an international peacekeeping operation, and expose their lack of public support through supervised elections. Solarz's cross-examination also made evident that Atkins was unprepared to support the kinds of U.S. actions that, in the absence of the UN plan, would be needed to counter the Khmer Rouge: the deployment of U.S. military forces to Cambodia or, at minimum, military assistance to Hun Sen's forces; a major aid program; and according diplomatic recognition to the State of Cambodia.

The Solarz-Atkins exchange was mirrored by Senate attacks on the matter of rumored battlefield cooperation between Prince Sihanouk's forces and the Khmer Rouge. These concerns sustained congressional pressure on the administration's policy for another six months, until the UN peace plan was formally ratified at the second session of the Paris Conference on Cambodia on October 23, 1991. The agreement finally enabled the noncommunist resistance leaders to disassociate themselves from the

Khmer Rouge, who were now boxed in by the settlement.[47] During the final Paris ministerial meeting, at which Foreign Minister Khieu Samphan signed the UN peace plan, Secretary Baker confronted the Khmer Rouge delegation with an affirmation of American support for international efforts to ensure protection of the human rights of the Cambodian people and to "bring to justice those responsible for the mass murders of the 1970s."[48]

---

47. Sihanouk formally declared the dissolution of the CGDK on February 3, 1990.

48. The United States was the only country, following the UNTAC settlement, to unilaterally take steps to bring the Khmer Rouge to justice. In April 1992 Senator Chuck Robb of Virginia introduced legislation that directed the State Department to establish an Office of Cambodian Genocide Investigation that would collect information on the Khmer Rouge's violent rule of the late 1970s. Such information would be the basis for eventual establishment of a national or international criminal tribunal that would prosecute the Khmer Rouge leadership for crimes against humanity and genocide. Such an office was established and collected material on the Khmer Rouge, in part with the assistance of the Cambodian government established after the UN-supervised elections of 1993. As of the end of 1999, however, the issue of establishing an *international* tribunal to bring surviving Khmer Rouge leaders to account was still opposed by Hun Sen, who had broken up the movement by offering individual Khmer Rouge leaders amnesty from prosecution in order to get them to rally to his government.

Building Consensus for the UN Settlement Plan

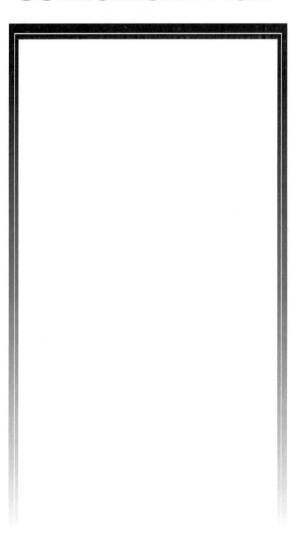

Building an *international* consensus for the UN plan, once published by the Perm Five in their framework agreement of August 1990, was relatively easy. The difficult part was getting the four Khmer factions to shift their conflict, as Secretary of State Baker liked to put it, "from the battlefield to the ballot box." In advancing this "internal" aspect of the UN plan, the United States played a secondary role. The Perm Five monitored negotiations with the four Khmer factions, which were managed largely by the cochairs of the Paris Conference, with Indonesia's Foreign Minister Alatas in the lead. In the year between early September 1990 and the same month in 1991, there were more than nine meetings involving the Khmer factions. These sessions intertwined the Perm Five consultations, the JIM process, and the Paris Conference leadership in an effort to define, in operational terms, how the Perm Five framework of August 1990 would be implemented.

Behind these consultations, indeed driving them, the powers of the communist world who were supporting the Khmer combatants as an extension of their own rivalries—the Russians, Chinese, and Vietnamese—were conducting their own bilateral diplomacy. Sino-Soviet relations had taken a major turn for the better in the late 1980s when Moscow reduced its troop deployments along the Sino-Soviet frontier. In May 1989 Gorbachev traveled to Beijing to normalize relations, and this summit was followed by a series of ministerial and subministerial encounters that progressively reduced Moscow's support for both Vietnam and Cambodia and brought Soviet diplomacy regarding Indochina into line with the Perm Five process.[49]

---

49. This Soviet diplomacy was conducted by Moscow's representative in the Perm Five negotiations, Deputy Foreign Minister Igor Rogachev. In late 1989 and early 1990 Rogachev was active in the region, holding talks with Hun Sen, the Vietnamese, and the Chinese. Moscow's clients were under increasing pressure to support a UN-managed settlement. In April 1990 Premier Li Peng of China visited Moscow, at which time Gorbachev announced more Soviet troop reductions in the Far East and major cutbacks in Soviet aid to Vietnam and the State of Cambodia. By the end of 1990 the Soviets were selling combat aircraft to China—an indication of how far the improvement in Sino-Soviet relations under Gorbachev had progressed. And in May 1991 China's senior leaders traveled to Moscow to sign a major agreement settling long-standing territorial disputes along the Sino-Soviet frontier. In August the Cambodia deal was essentially done.

The diplomatic activity involving the factions accelerated in early 1990, when the Indonesians, French, and Australians—as noted earlier—convened a third JIM meeting in Jakarta in late February. Their goal was to salvage the progress of the Paris Conference. The Khmer initially accepted the idea of an enhanced UN role in a settlement, but provocative proposals by Vietnamese foreign minister Thach on the issue of genocide repolarized the meeting. As JIM III collapsed, Gareth Evans expressed frustration at the squabbling factions; and Alatas, angered at Thach's disruptive intervention, concluded that the meeting had undercut any momentum remaining in the peace process.[50] Thach continued to play the spoiler role until a major leadership shake-up and policy realignment in his government led senior Vietnamese political leaders to "retire" the veteran diplomat in June 1991, sixteen months later, when Sino-Vietnamese relations were well on the way to full normalization.

Despite the continuing resistance of Hun Sen and the Vietnamese, the Perm Five consensus put heightened presssure on all the Khmer factions to accede to a UN-managed political settlement. In early September 1990, just two weeks after publication of the Perm Five framework agreement, Alatas convened another JIM session, and the factions agreed to form a twelve-member Supreme National Council.[51] Sihanouk absented himself from the meeting, however, in order to gain leverage for his claim to be the thirteenth member and chairman of the SNC. The prince and Hun Sen continued to spar for ten more months over the structure of the body, finally agreeing in early June 1991 to an arrangement with Sihanouk as president and Hun Sen as vice president.

Subsequent meetings of the SNC with representatives of the Perm Five, the JIM countries, and the Paris Conference were held in late September, November, and December 1990. The Australian Red Book helped to focus discussion on such operational aspects of the peace process as the

---

50. See Steven Erlanger, "Peace Talks on Cambodia Break Down," *New York Times*, March 1, 1990.

51. See Steven Erlanger, "Ending Talks, All Cambodian Parties Commit Themselves to UN Peace Plan," *New York Times*, September 10, 1990.

mandate of the UN transitional authority, the UN role in repatriating the Khmer refugees along the Thai border, and controlling the military forces. The participants also designed an electoral system based on a one-stage process of voting for lists of party candidates, rather than two stages of voting on the basis of either a proportional system or territorial constituencies. Yet the interchanges never came to closure. Hun Sen and the Vietnamese continued to resist UNTAC arrangements that would weaken the authority and structure of the State of Cambodia. Thach and Hun Sen dragged out the negotiations in hopes of rallying support for their position—even from the United States.

Most revealing of the underlying source of the stalemate was the outcome of a visit to Hanoi in early June 1990 by China's representative in the Perm Five process, Vice Foreign Minister Xu Dunxin. Press reports of this bilateral Chinese initiative to gain Vietnam's support for a Cambodia settlement were sketchy, but diplomatic circles were abuzz with the rumor that Foreign Minister Thach had gratuitously insulted the visiting Chinese envoy in an effort to keep the diplomacy deadlocked.[52]

Beginning in September 1990, however, with the Perm Five plan now public, senior Chinese and Vietnamese political leaders attempted to resolve their differences in a series of secret bilateral deliberations.[53] Thach was noticeably excluded from this high-level politicking; Beijing was rumored to have demanded the removal of the intensely nationalistic Thach as a condition for normalizing relations. At the Vietnamese Seventh Communist Party Congress in June 1991 Thach lost his seat on the Politburo, and he was retired from his position as foreign minister a month later at

---

52. See James Sterngold, "China Faults U.S. Shift on Cambodia," *New York Times,* July 19, 1990.

53. There may have been four secret meetings, the first of which was held in Chengdu, China, in early September 1990 between Vietnamese Communist Party leader Do Muoi and former prime minister Pham Van Dong and their Chinese counterparts, Jiang Zemin and Li Peng. See Lena Sun, "Leaders of Vietnam, China Held Secret Talks," *Washington Post,* September 19, 1990; Michael Leifer, "Cambodia: Beijing's New Role as Peacemaker," *International Herald Tribune,* July 16, 1991; and Jacques Bekaert, "China: New Focus for Vietnam," *Jane's Defence Weekly,* December 21, 1991.

a meeting of the National Assembly.[54] Within weeks, Sino-Vietnamese relations were fully normalized after more than a decade of political hostility and military conflict.

The end game of Sino-Vietnamese diplomacy affecting Cambodia was conducted by Xu Dunxin and his new Vietnamese counterpart, Nguyen Dy Nien, between July and September 1991. In late summer of 1991 rumors began to circulate in the press and diplomatic channels that Beijing and Hanoi were cooking up a "Red solution" to the Cambodia conflict. The concern was that they would agree to a settlement largely excluding the United Nations in favor of a power-sharing arrangement between the Pol Pot and Hun Sen factions of the Khmer communist movement.[55]

In fact, Beijing remained committed to the Perm Five process. The Chinese hosted an SNC meeting in Beijing in mid-July that created an SNC secretariat and formed a new Cambodian UN delegation, in anticipation of the fall meeting of the General Assembly. The delegation was headed by Prince Sihanouk and included representatives of the other political factions. A month later, the Perm Five, the ASEAN states, Laos, and Vietnam convened a full-dress SNC meeting in Pattaya, Thailand. The meeting produced agreement on the core "power" issue of the disposition of the military forces. Despite Sihanouk's public appeal that the factional armies be completely dismantled and reorganized,[56] the participants reached consensus on a formula proposed by Hun Sen of 70 percent disarmament, 30 percent cantonment under the supervision of a UN peacekeeping force, and an end to all foreign military assistance.[57] Hun Sen's concession to

---

54. Vietnam's new foreign minister, Nguyen Manh Cam, represented Hanoi at the concluding session of the Paris Conference on Cambodia three months later.

55. See Michael Richardson, "Asians Fear Deal on Cambodia as China-Vietnam Ties Warm," *International Herald Tribune*, August 7, 1991.

56. Kulachada Chaipipat and Yindee Lertcharoenchok, "Sihanouk Calls for Armies to Be Disbanded," *The Nation* (Bangkok), August 24, 1991.

57. Press rumors suggested that this formula for resolving the military issue had been worked out behind the scenes by the Chinese representative, Xu Dunxin, and his

this arrangement, which enabled him to maintain his military organization, was agreement to drop any reference to the Khmer Rouge's genocide in the section of the peace plan dealing with human rights.[58]

The August Pattaya meeting was significant because it revealed that final agreement among all the parties to the peace process was all but accomplished. The multilayered diplomacy was succeeding because the major protagonists in the Cold War, all permanent members of the UN Security Council, were determined to resolve their differences and exit Indochina. The Soviets and the Chinese, after three decades of bitter feuding and confrontation, were now working together; and the United States was able to coordinate policy on Indochina with both former adversaries. The Cold War was coming to an end.

An almost poignant example of the altered relations among the major powers was the Perm Five session at Pattaya on August 29. In a discussion of national commitments to the economic reconstruction of Cambodia, the Soviet representative, Igor Rogachev, bemoaned that he could not make an aid commitment on behalf of his government because "I'm not sure I have a country to represent." A coup against Gorbachev had split the Soviet leadership ten days earlier and the Baltic republics, Ukraine, and Byelorussia were voting for independence from Moscow. Dissolution of the Soviet Union was just four months away.[59]

Perhaps the most bizarre scene in this diplomatic end game was the celebratory banquet at Pattaya. Sihanouk was in an ebullient mood. The international community was about to give his country back to him. The prince, long famous for his musical interests, led the dinner orchestra in

---

Vietnamese counterpart, Nguyen Dy Nien. Rodney Tasker, "What Killing Fields?" *Far Eastern Economic Review,* September 12, 1991, 15.

58. "Khmers Agree on Dropping All References to Genocide," *Bangkok Post,* August 30, 1991.

59. See Bush and Scowcroft, *A World Transformed,* 518–561.

renditions of his original Khmer and French love songs. Elated, Sihanouk approached me and directed that I sing a song in celebration of the Perm Five's contribution to the peace process. Having little musical talent I resisted, saying I would perform only in the company of my Perm Five colleagues.[60] Not knowing an appropriate song that might conceivably be known to all five members of this unlikely diplomatic quintet, I suddenly remembered that the first anniversary of the Perm Five framework agreement was at hand and that Sihanouk's sixty-ninth birthday was only weeks away. I implored my British, Chinese, French, and Russian counterparts to join me on the stage for a collective rendition of—"Happy Birthday." For me the celebratory mood was chilled, however, by the ghoulish sight of Khmer Rouge delegates Khieu Samphan and Son Sen laughing at the diplomatic revelers in the crowded banquet room.

A final SNC meeting was convened by the Perm Five in New York in late September, on the eve of the forty-sixth UN General Assembly. The last major issue, the structure of the electoral process, was finally resolved in favor of a system of proportional representation that would give each faction a share of seats in the new national assembly according to its share of the popular vote on a province-by-province basis.[61] Four days later, Sihanouk called on President Bush, also in New York for the General Assembly session, to describe the all but complete peace process that, counting from the time of the Paris Conference in August 1989 had taken just over two years to construct.[62] A month later, on October 23, the

---

60. At this point in the diplomacy, France's Claude Martin had been replaced by Jean-David Levitte, and David Gilmore of Great Britain had been replaced by Robin McLaren. China's Xu Dunxin, Russia's Igor Rogachev, and I remained as the negotiators for our respective countries.

61. Paul Lewis, "Cambodians Reach Accord on Elections," *New York Times,* September 21, 1991. Hun Sen resisted the proportional system in favor of a territorial constituency-based system—which would have played to the strengths of his political organization throughout the country. This compromise was to be the basis of a major challenge by Hun Sen to the outcome of the May 1993 election.

62. Ever the provocateur, the prince told President Bush that he anticipated a Khmer Rouge victory in the elections.

second session of the Paris Conference on Cambodia ratified the agreement.

In retrospect, it is clear that the parallel and mutually reinforcing reconciliations of 1991 between Beijing and Moscow, and Beijing and Hanoi, made possible the fundamental political deals that enabled the Perm Five's peace plan for Cambodia to fall into place. Although the content of this bilateral diplomacy remains largely unknown to outside observers, subsequent developments make it evident that a major objective of all the communist parties was to end more than three decades of Sino-Soviet hostility and military confrontation. For the Chinese, this meant that Moscow was no longer trying to "encircle" China. For the Vietnamese, this meant the end of Moscow's diplomatic and military support and assistance programs, which had seen them through the war with the Americans in the 1960s and 1970s and their confrontation with the Chinese in the late 1970s and 1980s. Thus isolated, Hanoi had no recourse but to give up on Ho Chi Minh's dream of an Indochina Federation—of Vietnam as the hegemon over Laos and Cambodia—and to normalize relations with China on Beijing's terms.

Once the Vietnamese had reconciled with the Chinese, Hun Sen was under irresistable pressure from both Hanoi and Moscow to accept compromises that would make the peace process work. The Chinese were concurrently pressing the Khmer Rouge to compromise in the interest of the settlement. At the final SNC meetings there was no longer the impasse between "genocide" and "colonialism" but concentration on the central power issues of the military dispositions and the electoral system. Under the pressure of the major powers, Cambodia's factions moved their unresolved and probably irreconcilable differences, however reluctantly, from the killing fields to the UN-managed political process.

Exiting the
Vietnam Quagmire

An associated and by no means inconsequential aspect of the Cambodia negotiations was the matter of normalizing U.S.-Vietnam relations. This issue was organic to the politics of the Cambodia settlement, for it was Hanoi's Christmas day invasion of Cambodia in 1978 that had aborted at the last minute an effort by the Carter administration, led by Assistant Secretary of State Richard Holbrooke, to normalize relations.[63]

In the late 1970s Soviet-American relations were increasingly strained because of aggressive Soviet initiatives in many parts of the world, among them heightened military activities in Indochina and the invasion of Afghanistan on December 26, 1979. In this context, President Carter's National Security adviser, Zbigniew Brzezinski, convinced the president to shift the administration's foreign policy priorities in Asia to developing a strategic entente with China. By all evidence, Vietnam was coordinating its own initiatives with Moscow. Hanoi had signed a Treaty of Friendship and Cooperation with the Soviet Union in November 1978 that gave Moscow access to naval facilities at Da Nang and Cam Ranh Bay. In return, the Vietnamese received substantial Soviet aid, and they probably reached a secret understanding with the Soviets about political and military assistance if attacked by China. Hanoi's forces invaded Cambodia the day before Moscow invaded Afghanistan. President Carter put normalization with Vietnam on hold and proceeded rapidly to complete the full normalization of relations with China.[64]

Despite Vietnam's strategic dependence on the Soviet Union in the 1980s, the Reagan administration maintained a low-level dialogue with Hanoi

---

63. Normalization might have been accomplished in the fall of 1978, but the Vietnamese pressed for war reparations, to which the Carter administration would not agree. The negotiations between Holbrooke and then–deputy foreign minister Nguyen Co Thach dragged on in New York until evidence that Vietnam was preparing to invade Cambodia led the U.S. to disengage from the talks in December. See Becker, *When the War Was Over,* 385–402.

64. Zbigniew Brzezinski, *Power and Principle: Memoirs of the National Security Adviser, 1977–1981* (New York: Farrar, Straus, and Giroux, 1983), 403–414. See also Becker, *When the War Was Over,* 401–402; and Frederick Z. Brown, *Second Chance: The United States and Indochina in the 1990s* (New York: Council on Foreign Relations, 1989), 18–36.

because of unresolved concerns about the fate of American servicemen still missing from the war years. The Vietnamese expressed interest in improving relations with the United States, but were unwilling to agree to American proposals for systematic resolution of a number of humanitarian concerns. By the end of the decade, however, the Vietnamese faced increasingly serious domestic economic difficulties and failing support from the Soviet Union. These unfavorable circumstances, in combination with unrelenting pressure from the Chinese, gave us some influence in bringing the Vietnamese to support the Perm Five settlement plan for Cambodia, although the primary factor, as already described, was Hanoi's decision in 1991 to normalize relations with China.

For the United States, dealing with Vietnam carried all the burdens of a disastrous war and diplomatic betrayal. Following Hanoi's successful military reunification of Vietnam in 1975, the primary issue in Washington's Vietnam policy was to gain the fullest possible accounting of the fate of more than 2,300 servicemen missing from the war years—the "missing in action" or MIA question. There were persistent rumors that live American POWs—military prisoners—were still being held captive in secret camps in Vietnam and Laos. The POW/MIA issues had considerable domestic political force. The National League of Families, representing the relatives of missing servicemen, was actively pressing both American and Vietnamese leaders for resolution of these matters; its efforts were supported by many of the main line veterans groups. The league's executive director, Ann Mills Griffiths, was directly involved in efforts of the Reagan and Bush administrations to engage Hanoi in a process of POW/MIA accounting. This issue was the focus of a number of diplomatic initiatives from Washington beginning in 1977 and, after a hiatus at the turn of the decade, continuing through the 1980s.[65] After Hanoi's invasion of Cambodia in late 1978, the issue of a political settlement for the country based on the withdrawal of Vietnam's army of occupation added

---

65. For a detailed history of U.S.-Vietnam relations in the 1970s and 1980s, see Childress and Solarz, "Vietnam," 88–107.

a further burden to the unpromising, if not receding, prospects for normalizing U.S.-Vietnam relations.

During the 1980s the Reagan administration made a number of proposals to the Vietnamese to establish an orderly regime of field investigations that would resolve individual POW/MIA cases on a "humanitarian" basis—that is, free of political conditions. In 1987 President Reagan sent a delegation to Hanoi headed by a special representative, former chairman of the Joint Chiefs of Staff General John Vessey, to seek agreement to the field investigations and the repatriation of remains held by the Vietnamese. This and other efforts, however, were compromised by unacceptable political conditions put forward by Hanoi, which was represented in its dealings with the United States by the familiar diplomatic figure and now foreign minister Nguyen Co Thach.

My first contact with Thach was at the Paris Conference in August 1989. An official in the Vietnamese delegation approached a member of the U.S. negotiating team and inquired whether I would be interested in a meeting with the foreign minister. I reported this approach back to Washington and was told that I was authorized to hold a meeting *only* if the Vietnamese made a specific request for such an encounter. It was clear that there was limited enthusiasm in the Bush administration for engaging Hanoi on political issues. There was little confidence in the reliability of the wily Thach, and the Vietnamese delegation's performance at the Paris Conference gave us little evidence of common ground with Hanoi on the terms of a Cambodian settlement. Moreover, a number of senior administration officials who had dealt with the Vietnamese in the early 1970s, as the Nixon administration sought to end the war through negotiations, felt little sympathy for a government that had violated the Paris Accords of 1973 by taking over South Vietnam by force of arms.

The Vietnamese proposal for a meeting was somewhat ambiguous. The initiative had come from them; yet the phrasing, so familiar in Asian terms, was cast so as to make the American side look like the *demandeur*. My judgment was that an unpublicized encounter might have some future value as the negotiations played out and that a meeting would give us the opportunity to state directly the administration's terms for improving relations.[66] Thus, the day after the Paris Conference was "suspended," four members of my delegation and I called on Foreign Minister Thach at the Vietnamese embassy on rue Boileau. The forty-five-minute encounter was stiff and unenlightening. Thach's objective, apparently, was to hear if this newcomer in a long line of American interlocutors had something unexpected to say, and perhaps to create the impression in diplomatic circles that Washington was now talking to Hanoi about Cambodia. I used the occasion, as instructed, to stress that our relations could be normalized only in the context of Vietnam's support for a Cambodia settlement and with resolution of our POW/MIA concerns.

I left Paris and returned to Washington via New York in order to accept an invitation from former president Nixon to an informal dinner at his residence in northern New Jersey. The purpose of the event was to brief him and a small group of friends on the results of the Paris Conference. Nixon was intensely interested in the diplomatic byplay at Paris given the preoccupation of his administration with Vietnam and Cambodia during the war years. The former president was particularly concerned about the breakdown in Sino-American relations after Tiananmen and seemed pleased to hear of the cooperative dealings I had had with the Chinese at Paris. He did not comment on my uneventful meeting with Thach, but later expressed "outrage" at the Bush administration's plan to normalize relations with Vietnam.[67] His views had considerable support within the government and from a number of veterans organizations.

---

66. President Bush had signaled Vietnam in his inaugural address in January 1989 that cooperation on POW/MIA issues would remove a major obstacle to improving relations. On November 17, 1989, Deputy Assistant Secretary of State David Lambertson testified before the House Subcommittee on Asian and Pacific Affairs that normalization of Vietnamese-American relations was directly linked to a Cambodia settlement, while the "pace and scope" of normalization would depend on Hanoi's cooperation on POW/MIA accountability.

67. See Monica Crowley, *Nixon in Winter* (New York: Random House, 1998), 272. This oral history recounts that within two years Nixon reversed his opposition to normalizing relations with Vietnam in the interest of promoting change within the still-communist state. See also Richard Nixon, *Beyond Peace* (New York: Random House, 1994), 137.

There was no immediate follow-up by the Bush administration on my
encounter with Thach. The Vietnamese continued to block progress on a
Cambodia settlement. In the winter and spring months of 1990, however, pressure began to build in the Congress for improving relations
with Vietnam. In mid-February the Aspen Institute's "Indochina Forum"
hosted one in a series of meetings between American businessmen and
congressional leaders and Vietnamese officials, this one in Bali, Indonesia. The encounter reflected growing private-sector interest in developing commercial relations with Vietnam, as well as the concern of Vietnam
War veterans in Congress such as Senator Chuck Robb of Virginia with
coming to terms with the former adversary.[68]

Congressional pressures to deal with Vietnam increased in the spring as
intelligence reporting from Cambodia heightened concerns about possible military cooperation between Prince Sihanouk's forces and the
Khmer Rouge.[69] As detailed earlier, these concerns were expressed in late
June and early July in a letter from sixty-six senators to Secretary of State
Baker. The lawmakers pressed the administration to modify in a fundamental way its Cambodia policy, urging among other things the establishment of a dialogue with Hanoi. In response, the administration not
only backed away from Sihanouk's political coalition with the Khmer
Rouge, but also announced the intention to initiate direct discussions
with both Hanoi and Phnom Penh.

---

68. See Michael Vatikiotis, "Testing the Waters," *Far Eastern Economic Review,* March 1,
1990, 19.

69. One of the more unique aspects of U.S. government management of foreign policy
is that, on occasion, midlevel intelligence officials can collaborate with congressional staff
to "leak" information to the press so as to build pressures against an administration's
policy. The more controversial the policy, the stronger the incentive of those who disagree
with it to leak. This was the case in the matter of occasional field reports that suggested
the possibility of battlefield cooperation between Khmer Rouge and FUNCINPEC
military units. (See, for example, Clifford Krauss, "U.S. Weighs Shift on Cambodia Policy,"
New York Times, July 7, 1990.) We spent considerable time and attention evaluating such
field reports, which, if true, would have required the administration to cut off aid to the
noncommunist resistance.

This policy shift was implemented the following month. My deputy, Kenneth Quinn, met with Vietnam's permanent representative to the United Nations, Trinh Xuan Lang, in early August. At the end of the month I met with Thach's deputy, Vice Foreign Minister Le Mai, to lay the groundwork for a meeting the following month in New York between Secretary Baker and Foreign Minister Thach.

The Baker-Thach encounter occurred on September 27 as the UN General Assembly was convening. The ever-manipulative Thach set the tone for the discussion by presenting Baker, at the outset of the meeting, a copy of Paul Samuelson's classic text *Economics*—which had been translated into Vietnamese! Thach commented that the text was guiding his country toward market-oriented economic reforms. He added, provocatively, that Samuelson's analysis helped him identify "loopholes" in U.S. law that would enable the Bush administration to lift its trade embargo with his country. Thach also urged an end to the administration's opposition to International Monetary Fund and World Bank loans to Vietnam, pleading that U.S. policies were only stiffening the resistance of unspecified "hard-liners" in his country to improving bilateral relations. Baker countered by stressing the need to overcome political resistance in the United States to normalization. He said that Vietnam could facilitate progress by supporting the just-published Perm Five framework agreement for settling the Cambodia conflict and resolving the POW/MIA issue. Accommodating congressional pressure, the secretary invited Thach to make a one-day visit to Washington for discussions with General John Vessey and Ann Mills Griffiths of the National League of Families and to meet with interested senators from the Foreign Relations Committee.

Following the Baker-Thach encounter and the foreign minister's visit to Washington, there was another hiatus in contacts with the Vietnamese as both Hanoi and Phnom Penh resisted implementation of the Perm Five plan. Yet pressures again built in Congress for normalization, driven by new reports of military cooperation between Sihanouk's forces and the Khmer Rouge. This time the administration responded by developing a comprehensive game plan that incorporated all the outstanding issues affecting U.S.-Vietnam normalization.

The administration's recast policy was publicly dubbed the "road map." It was designed as a four-stage process of mutually reinforcing confidence-building steps that would give Hanoi the political and economic benefits it was seeking in return for cooperation on the Cambodia settlement and in POW/MIA accounting. If implemented, we calculated, Vietnam's cooperation would help dissipate the enduring domestic climate of distrust and hostility and enable the two countries to normalize relations over approximately a two-year period.[70]

The plan itself had been formulated in an atmosphere of considerable bureaucratic tension. There was deep disagreement between those who expected Hanoi to resolve the POW/MIA issues *before* improving relations and those who saw steps to improving relations as a way of eliciting Vietnamese cooperation on POW/MIA accounting—as well as a useful response to congressional pressures. Feuding over some of the road map's terms persisted until the very minute before I presented the new policy to Ambassador Lang in New York on April 9. We then reinforced the initiative by announcing on April 25 a $1 million program of prosthetics assistance to Vietnamese wounded during the war.

Hanoi reacted to the road map policy by neither accepting its terms nor rejecting the concept of a step-by-step process of improving relations. Thach publicly criticized the linkage inherent in the staged approach, but otherwise was rather passive in his response. What we only vaguely sensed at the time was that the Vietnamese leadership was in the midst of a fundamental reassessment of its domestic and foreign policies. As described earlier, a Communist Party congress in June produced a major leadership shake-up that saw "conservatives" like Mai Chi Tho, as well as Foreign Minister Thach, lose their Politburo and ministerial positions.

---

70. See my testimony before the Senate Subcommittee on East Asian and Pacific Affairs, "Vietnam: The Road Ahead," April 25, 1991.

This dramatic development, which was influenced by the growing political crisis in the communist world, led Hanoi to finally support the UN settlement plan for Cambodia and accept China's terms for normalizing bilateral relations.

For the United States, Hanoi's signature on the Cambodia peace plan in Paris on October 23 met the key requirement of phase one of the road map. Consequently, I had a third meeting with Vice Foreign Minister Le Mai in New York on November 21, during which we established working groups to review the various issues associated with normalization. Three months later, as the first UNTAC contingents were establishing themselves in Cambodia, I traveled to Hanoi (as well as to Phnom Penh and Vientiane) with a delegation that included officials from the Department of Defense and Ann Mills Griffiths of the National League of Families. Meetings with the Vietnamese produced an agreement to institutionalize the long-proposed system of field investigations for systematic POW/MIA accounting.

Establishment of U.S.-Vietnam diplomatic relations was to take three more years. Hanoi abided by the terms of the Cambodia settlement and heightened its cooperation in POW/MIA accounting activities, but weak domestic support for improving relations with Hanoi, the forceful assertions of veterans groups that the Vietnamese were not doing all they could to repatriate war remains, and the transition from the Bush to the Clinton administrations dragged out further progress specified by the road map strategy. Congressional hearings on POW/MIA issues in 1991–92, promoted by Vietnam War veterans Senators John Kerry, John McCain, and Bob Smith, helped to broaden political support for normalization. The urgings of the senators, in combination with pressures from the American business community, finally moved the Clinton administration to establish diplomatic relations with Vietnam in the summer of 1995.

This was not full normalization, in that a number of significant issues incorporated in the road map, especially Most Favored Nation trading status for Vietnam, remained unresolved. Yet two decades after the end of the Vietnam War, with the Cold War receding into history, the United States had substantially disengaged from the affairs of Indochina.

The Playout:
Who Won? Who Lost?

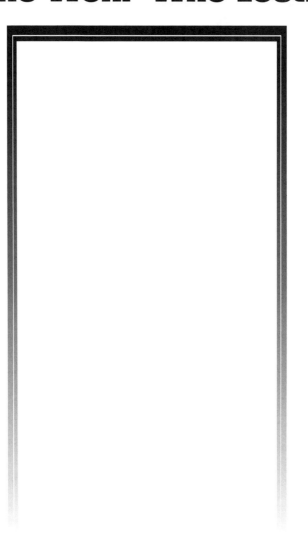

The process of *implementing* the United Nations peace plan for Cambodia is a story in itself and is not directly relevant to the purposes of this assessment.[71] But it is worth closing the circle on key issues explored in this reconstruction of the diplomacy underlying the Cambodia settlement by making some summary observations about the degree to which the various parties to the process attained their objectives.

The United Nations was a vehicle for the settlement, not a primary player. Yet in the history of international peace operations, the UN role in the peace process for Cambodia is likely to stand out as a signal success in facilitating multilateral diplomacy and then competently managing a peace plan. The UNTAC operation was the first and largest of its kind in UN history. Despite the challenges of operating in uncharted waters, the UN civil administration, along with a military contingent of 16,000 troops, was able to establish a relatively stable and secure environment for elections, which were held in May 1993. Despite Khmer Rouge efforts to disrupt the elections through acts of violence and intimidation, some 90 percent of those registered to vote did so. The balloting produced a plurality victory for Prince Sihanouk and his FUNCINPEC party, which gained 45 percent of the vote relative to 38 percent for Hun Sen and his Cambodian People's Party. The winners in the election then organized a Constituent Assembly that drafted a constitution establishing Cambodia as a parliamentary democracy. In September Sihanouk signed the new constitution into law and was once again enthroned as king of his country.

Given the deep concerns in many quarters that the peace agreement might enable the Khmer Rouge to regain power, it was especially significant

---

71. The best accounts of UNTAC's performance can be found in Michael W. Doyle, *UN Peacekeeping in Cambodia: UNTAC's Civil Mandate* (London and Boulder, Colo.: Lynne Rienner Publishers/International Peace Academy, 1995); Trevor Findlay, *Cambodia: The Legacy and Lessons of UNTAC*, SIPRI Research Report no. 9 (Oxford, England: Oxford University Press, 1995); Nassrine Azimi, comp., *The United Nations Transitional Authority in Cambodia (UNTAC): Debriefing and Lessons* (London: Kluwer Law International, 1995); United Nations, *The United Nations and Cambodia: 1991–1995* (New York: United Nations, 1995); and Sorpong Peou, *Conflict Neutralization in the Cambodia War: From Battlefield to Ballot-Box* (Kuala Lumpur: Oxford University Press, 1997).

that Pol Pot and his forces ultimately absented themselves from the settlement process. In June 1992 the Khmer Rouge refused to submit their troops to the demobilization process (as was required by the UN agreement, which Khieu Samphan had signed), and in January 1993 they announced they would boycott the elections. Thus the Khmer Rouge avoided a test of public opinion and also maintained their military capability, which they could use to challenge the government from bases in western and northwest Cambodia that had been untouched by UNTAC.

The ensuing five years saw some fighting between the Khmer Rouge and government forces. But in circumstances of a military standoff, the government succeeded in dissipating much of the Khmer Rouge's military strength through an amnesty program that pulled away many of the peasants and lower-level military personnel who had been attracted to or coerced into their service in the border enclaves. A complex, subterranean web of negotiations developed between Hun Sen, Ranariddh, and the various Khmer Rouge leaders, who were spread out in separated base areas along the Thai-Cambodia border. This led to conflicts and defections among the senior leaders over issues of economics and political strategy.

In the fall of 1996 Ieng Sary and his troops were granted amnesty by the government. Hun Sen presided over a formal "welcoming" ceremony at Pailin, where Ieng Sary continues to live with other Khmer Rouge leaders in secure comfort through control of gem and logging exports. In the spring of 1998, Pol Pot dispatched an assassination squad to the border enclave of his defense minister, Son Sen, who was murdered along with his wife, children, and grandchildren in a particularly brutal slaying that seems to have been motivated by policy disagreements over the amnesty program.

Pol Pot was subsequently arrested by other Khmer Rouge leaders, who subjected "brother number one" to a televised show trial before the world in order to discredit him and distance themselves from the dreaded leader of the auto-genocide of the late 1970s. Pol Pot died—or was murdered—

a few months later, a sick and isolated old man, never having faced international justice for the violence of his rule.[72]

In late 1998 Khieu Samphan and Nuon Chea defected to the government, which accorded them a curiously well-publicized tour of Cambodia before they returned to live in the safe haven of Pailin.[73] And in May 1999, Duch, the notorious warden of Tuol Sleng prison, where more than 16,000 were tortured to death, was discovered to be a Christian convert living in western Cambodia.[74]

Ta Mok "the butcher" was the only senior Khmer Rouge leader to be incarcerated for his role in the violence of the 1970s. He was captured in March 1999 and awaits trial with a number of second-rank officials of the movement.[75]

Thus, as hoped for in the Bush administration's design of the peace process, the Khmer Rouge movement imploded. The leadership turned in on itself in a spasm of the self-destructive violence and factionalism that has characterized so much of the movement's history. And while some leaders and their troops continue to control the Pailin area, as of late 1999 Ankar—the organization—has lost its ability to function as a coherent national military or political force.

The outcome of the UNTAC-managed political process is no less convoluted and full of intrigue than the fate of the Khmer Rouge. In a particularly

72. A dramatic and detailed account of Pol Pot's demise will be found in Nate Thayer, *Sympathy for the Devil: Living Dangerously in Cambodia, a Foreign Correspondent's Story* (New York: Viking Press, 1999).

73. Hun Sen welcomed the two in Phnom Penh on December 29, 1998, saying that "bygones should be bygones," but King Sihanouk publicly opposed granting them amnesty and they "retreated" to Pailin.

74. Seth Mydans, "70s' Torturer in Cambodia Now 'Doing God's Work,'" *New York Times,* May 2, 1999.

75. Seth Mydans, "Of Top Khmer Rouge, Only One Awaits Judgment," *New York Times,* March 14, 1999.

obscure development, Hun Sen and Cambodian People's Party, who were relegated to second-rank status in the elections of 1993, used the threat of secession by Prince Chakrapong to blackmail their way into the government.[76] Sihanouk negotiated a compromise to avert civil war by creating a dual ministerial government. Prince Ranariddh was designated first prime minister and Hun Sen second prime minister. This uneasy coalition endured for four years, amid continuing political machinations involving members of the royal family, Hun Sen, and various Khmer Rouge leaders. In July 1997—in anticipation of the elections of 1998— this coalition broke down. Hun Sen established full control of the government by driving Ranariddh and other FUNCINPEC leaders out of the government through force of arms.

A second round of internationally supervised elections in June 1998 again elicited strong public participation. Hun Sen gained 41 percent of the vote and Ranariddh 32 percent, requiring formation of another coalition government. And again, King Sihanouk had to intervene to negotiate a political arrangement, this time instituting Hun Sen as the sole prime minister and Ranariddh as president of the National Assembly.

Today, in late 1999, Cambodians live in a state of uneasy peace. The political institutions created by the UN-managed settlement have given a measure of stability to a society whose population and institutions were ravaged over three decades by war, revolution, and political violence. Yet the popularly elected government created by the 1993 elections coexists in a state of tandem fragility with the Leninist Cambodian People's Party, which continues to use intimidation and violence to limit the emergence of any significant organized political opposition. The royal establishment is still needed to overcome the powerful factional tendencies of the political class; yet with King Sihanouk in poor health and uncertainty about his successor, Cambodia's politics face a future beclouded by an elite culture of violence and corruption. Only continuing international pressure

---

76. See Becker, *When the War Was Over*, 514–515.

to maintain an open political process is likely to prevent Cambodia from succumbing to a state of corrupted one-party authoritarian rule.

Despite this gloomy prognosis for the future, the United Nations substantially fulfilled its mandate to bring peace to Cambodia. The country was given the opportunity, and the burden, of shaping its own destiny as an independent state. The evolution of Cambodia's domestic political institutions established by UNTAC no doubt falls short of the hopes of the international community, but the issue that must be addressed is what level of international intervention, and for what length of time, is appropriate to a sovereign country.

As for the five permanent members of the Security Council, their success in constructing the August 1990 framework agreement reflected a rare measure of common purpose at a unique moment in history. The Cold War was coming to an end; the Soviet Union, led by Mikhail Gorbachev, wanted normal relations with both China and the United States; China wanted a stable Southeast Asia to support its plans for economic development; and the United States and China, despite Tiananmen, were seeking to maintain a cooperative relationship. France was seeking to reestablish for itself a position of some influence in its former colonies of Cambodia and Vietnam. In sum, all the major powers wanted to pacify a region that had been a cockpit of international conflict for more than a century.[77] The UN Security Council proved to be an effective vehicle by which to achieve this pacification, even though the politics that made it possible were conducted in secret, bilateral negotiations between Moscow, Beijing, and Hanoi.

With the perspective of six years since the elections of 1993, it appears that of all the major powers, China achieved the greatest gains from the Cambodia settlement. A sensitive strategic area on China's southern

---

77. The British, who played a constructive role in the Perm Five process, had no significant involvement in Southeast Asia at this time and no specific objectives in the negotiations other than to avoid a costly UN settlement.

frontier was stabilized and freed of the influence of longtime rivals. Beijing was able to use the settlement to undermine Vietnam's hopes to organize a condominium over Cambodia and Laos. It unburdened itself of support for the Khmer Rouge and in recent years has come to terms with the predominant political force in postsettlement Cambodia—Hun Sen and the Cambodian People's Party. Given Beijing's positive relations with Burma and Thailand as well, China is positioned today to exercise significant political influence throughout the tier of states on its southern frontier, if not more broadly in Southeast Asia.

France failed to achieve its strategic objective of using the settlement process to reestablish for itself significant influence in Cambodia and Vietnam. Although Paris made a major contribution to the diplomacy of the Cambodia settlement, its effort to reestablish a significant presence in its former colonies has not succeeded. In the midst of the Perm Five negotiations, French diplomats were rumored to be rummaging through government warehouses in search of a throne on which to reseat Sihanouk—a reprise of their enthronement of the prince in 1941. But in the 1990s *les temps* were *perdue*. Sihanouk was dependent on Chinese power and on the United Nations coalition that was bringing him back to a position of leadership. In 1992, a year before the UN-supervised elections, Paris reestablished an Alliance Française in Phnom Penh to reinstitute French-language instruction.[78] But the effort had little success as Cambodia's younger generation, as with the Vietnamese, was seeking to learn a new lingua franca—English. Today France is neither a major investor nor trading country in the economies of Indochina.[79]

For the states of ASEAN, and especially its diplomatic leader, Foreign Minister Ali Alatas of Indonesia, the Cambodia settlement was a major

---

78. The formal name of this reconstituted French cultural presence was Centre de Cooperation Culturelle et Linguistique (CCCL). The "Alliance" name was not used for lack of a counterpart Cambodian organization with which to ally.

79. A senior French diplomat confided to me in 1998 that his country would have been better served by trying to rebuild influence in the region through economic measures rather than by focusing on cultural activities such as French-language instruction.

achievement. ASEAN played a major, constructive role in the diplomacy of the settlement, and the outcome stabilized a part of the region that had been a major source of instability, through great power interventions, war, and refugee flows, for more than a century. In 1995 ASEAN agreed to bring all three states of Indochina, along with Burma (Myanmar), into the organization, in fulfillment of the original conception of ASEAN as an all-inclusive regional association. Vietnam was admitted in 1995; the other states were to be admitted in 1997, but because of Hun Sen's coup of July 1997 their admission was delayed until April 1999.

Vietnam, from one perspective, was a loser in the Cambodia settlement in that it had to abandon Ho Chi Minh's dream of creating under its aegis a federation of three socialist states of Indochina. Yet in a larger sense the country gained significant benefits: Cambodia was neutralized as a security threat; relations with China were normalized; and the country and the region were at last unburdened of interventions by outside powers. Vietnam was freed to make its own future.

Australia and Japan, two active regional players in the settlement, had rather differing effects on the process. Canberra, through the efforts of Foreign Minister Gareth Evans, had a significant impact in building support for the United Nations peace plan; and an Australian military professional, General John Sanderson, made a distinguished contribution to UNTAC as commander of the UN military contingent. Tokyo's diplomatic involvement in the diplomacy, through collaboration with the Thai in 1990, was a diversion from the United Nations process; yet in subsequently supporting UNTAC with peacekeeping forces, Japan was able to make one of its first contributions to a United Nations peace process. And with Hun Sen's emergence as the predominant political figure in postsettlement Cambodia, Japan has been able to pursue its economic interests in the country with a "friendly" government.

For the United States, the outcome of the settlement achieved all the policy objectives laid out at the Paris Conference in 1989 by Secretary of State

Baker: the verified withdrawal of all Vietnamese forces; the safe return of the Khmer refugees in Thailand; and a successful, UN-managed political process that established a government legitimated by popular vote. Moreover, the self-destruction of the Khmer Rouge laid to rest the issue that had so rent the domestic American political debate surrounding the settlement. Thus, the basic policy judgment that had shaped the Bush administration's negotiation of a UN-managed settlement—undermining the Khmer Rouge by enveloping them in a process that would contain their military forces and subjecting them to the judgment of Khmer popular opinion—was ultimately vindicated. To be sure, that positive outcome came about because the Khmer Rouge leaders themselves withdrew from the settlement process and subsequently fell apart as a coherent political organization. But the fact was that this violence-prone movement could not survive in isolation from outside support or in the open political environment created by the international community through UNTAC and the popularly elected government that emerged from the settlement.

That said, uncertainty persists over international and domestic Cambodian efforts to bring the remnant Khmer Rouge leadership to justice for the auto-genocide of the 1970s.[80] Moreover, violence and intimidation continue to distort Cambodia's politics. The country today has not attained the measure of political democracy or economic revival that was hoped for. Continuing violence and corruption speak to the difficulty of transforming the political culture of an entrenched elite, as well as the importance of sustaining international influence in the follow-through phase of a peace process.[81]

An adjunct of the Cambodia settlement for the United States was substantial progress in normalizing relations with Vietnam. Although the

---

80. See Barbara Crossette, "U.S. Seeks to Break Impasse Blocking Khmer Rouge Trials," *New York Times*, October 20, 1999.

81. See Fen Osler Hampson, *Nurturing Peace: Why Peace Settlements Succeed or Fail* (Washington, D.C.: United States Institute of Peace Press, 1996).

wounds of the Vietnam War have yet to fully heal for either Americans or Vietnamese, there has been a measure of reconciliation through the still-incomplete process of POW/MIA accounting, the establishment of diplomatic and economic relations, and a range of humanitarian assistance programs that have brought together former adversaries. In both the Cambodia and Vietnam settlements, the United States attained a constructive exit to one of the most bitter and costly conflicts of the Cold War years, as well as a successful venture in international diplomacy.

Conclusion:
The United States as an
International Mediator

What lessons can we learn from the Cambodia settlement about successful international mediation in support of a peace process? Three broad themes stand out in this reconstruction of the negotiations of 1989–91: the issue of "ripeness," of whether the political environment is favorable to building support for a settlement; the importance of leadership in constructing a consensus; and the element of serendipity, of unexpected developments that influence the balance of factors in support of, or in opposition to, a settlement.

Are Circumstances "Ripe" for a Settlement?

> *A helmsman must learn to ride with the tide,*
> *or else he will be swamped by the waves.*
> —Zhou Enlai to Henry Kissinger, 1971

It took more than a decade to construct a peace process for Cambodia, and the efforts of the United Nations and individual countries in the 1980s occurred in circumstances that were not favorable to successful diplomacy. Late in the decade, however, as the Soviet Union began to withdraw its support for Vietnam and the Hun Sen government in Phnom Penh, circumstances began to change. The Paris Conference of August 1989 also took place before political forces in support of a settlement had fully "ripened,"[82] yet the diplomacy at the Kléber Conference Centre, in combination with the prior efforts of Indonesia in the JIM process, contributed to building a broad international consensus in support of what evolved into the UN settlement plan. There was thus substantial "prenegotiation" that created a multilayered regional and international coalition in support of a settlement.

---

82. The concept of political "ripeness" has been developed by Professor I. William Zartman. See his *Elusive Peace: Negotiating an End to Civil Wars* (Washington, D.C.: Brookings Institution, 1995), esp. 18; also, Louis Krieberg, "Timing and the Initiation of De-escalation Moves," in *Negotiation Theory and Practice*, ed. J. William Breslin and Jeffrey Z. Rubin (Cambridge, Mass.: Harvard University Law School, Program on Negotiations, 1991), 223–231.

The one element in the coalition that never fully "ripened" was the core of the conflict—the rivalries among the Khmer political factions. The international community essentially imposed a political settlement on Hun Sen and the Khmer Rouge. Only Prince Sihanouk and Son Sann gained from the process. The subsequent deterioration in Cambodia's politics following the successful election of 1993 underlines the fact that without broad *internal* support for the terms of a settlement, the investment of the international community in a peace agreement can easily be lost without effective mid- to long-term follow-through. There are almost never rapid and costless solutions to long-standing, bitter conflicts such as the one that ravaged Cambodia. If the international community seeks only a quick exit from such a conflict, it is unlikely to create a stable peace. One of the prices of peace building in the post–Cold War world is sustained international action in support of a conflict resolution process. The costs of such action are usually far less than continuing warfare, yet mustering the international political will for such follow-through—especially in the face of competing demands for attention and resources— is a major challenge.

The Importance of Leadership

The United States was one of several countries that took on the risks and burdens of leadership in bringing peace to Cambodia. Indonesia, France, and Australia, at different times in the decade-long effort, made major contributions as well. The United States was an important catalyzer of the diplomatic process in the year from September 1989 through August 1990 as it structured the Perm Five negotiations that produced a framework agreement for a UN-managed peace process. The U.S. effort drew strength from the JIM meetings and the Paris Conference. It was facilitated by the various mechanisms of the United Nations, which provided neutral ground for the Security Council consultations and political backing through votes of the Security Council and the General Assembly in support of the settlement plan. And the plan was implemented with remarkable effectiveness through the office of the UN secretary-general.

The United Nations thus gave effect to the international consensus for a Cambodian settlement. Yet the political weight and initiative of the United States in pressing for a UN-managed peace process prevented dissipation of the progress made at the Paris Conference of 1989 and in JIM-centered diplomacy. It also preempted the possibility of a settlement worked out bilaterally between the Chinese and the Vietnamese-Russians—the feared "Red solution." U.S. leadership, and the United Nations, gave the Russians, Chinese, and Vietnamese a relatively neutral process by which to back away from decades of confrontation.

The particular challenge for the Bush administration, as it would be for any U.S. government taking a significant initiative in international diplomacy, was to build and sustain domestic political support, especially in Congress. Internal political considerations impelled the administration to take the lead in promoting a settlement of the Cambodia conflict, yet congressional "symbolic politics" surrounding the effort—the concern to prevent another genocide, and the political imperative of being *seen* to be doing so—were in constant tension with the mechanics of constructing a realistic settlement process that would control the Khmer Rouge.

At several points in the two-year period between the fall of 1989 and the signing of the peace plan in Paris in October 1991, congressional opposition might have undercut the administration's diplomacy by cutting off assistance to Prince Sihanouk and Son Sann. When the political issues in a settlement are highly divisive, and when the uncertainties of politics—the diplomatic equivalent of the "fog of war"—allow for profound differences in judgment, much of the business of *international* diplomacy in fact becomes management of domestic *political* byplay.

In that effort, senior administration leadership of the diplomacy—by the president and secretary of state—becomes critical to the work of designated negotiators, whether they be a presidential special representative or an assistant secretary of state. Such support entails incurring the significant political risk that a negotiation might not succeed—as well as the risks and costs of inaction, of *not* taking the lead. Support from congressional leaders is also critical to building bipartisan executive-legislative support. In the case of the Cambodia settlement and the associated process of normalizing relations with Vietnam, the support of Congressman Stephen Solarz and a number of senatorial Vietnam War veterans was critical in preventing a fundamental split between Congress and the administration.

Serendipity

In the conduct of diplomacy, political factors, policy agendas, and events influencing the evolution of a negotiation are often incalculable, unknown, or unanticipated. The real world of international politics is full of surprises, and leaders facing unpromising or uncertain circumstances may well seek to drag out a negotiation in hopes that some unexpected development will enhance prospects for success. Evaluating the "correlation of forces" influencing a political process is a major leadership skill; playing for time in hopes of the intervention of some unexpected or hoped-for development is the instinct of a risk taker.

In the politics of the Cambodia settlement, serendipity played an important role in the ultimate success of the negotiations of 1989–91. The unexpected factor, only vaguely anticipated at the time of the first Paris Conference, was the collapse of the Soviet Union, which brought with it pressures on Vietnam to accept the UN settlement plan and to normalize relations with China. Had Moscow not been forced by its own economic and political straits to withdraw support from Vietnam and the Hun Sen government, it is doubtful that the Perm Five negotiations would have come to closure. And had the Vietnamese leadership not fundamentally shifted its policies in mid-1991, it is equally doubtful that Hanoi would have acceded to Beijing's terms for normalization, which included support for the UN settlement in Cambodia.

Yet such fortuitous developments *did* occur, helping to bring to fruition the collective efforts of the international community to bring peace to Cambodia.

Bibliography

Azimi, Nassrine, comp. *The United Nations Transitional Authority in Cambodia (UNTAC): Debriefing and Lessons.* London: Kluwer Law International, 1995.

Becker, Elizabeth. *America's Vietnam War: A Narrative History.* New York: Clarion Books, 1992.

———. *When the War Was Over: Cambodia and the Khmer Rouge Revolution.* New York: Perseus Books, Public Affairs, 1998.

Berry, Ken. *Cambodia from Red to Blue: Australia's Initiative for Peace.* Sydney, Australia: Allen and Unwin, 1998.

Brown, Frederick Z. *Second Chance: The United States and Indochina in the 1990s.* New York: Council on Foreign Relations, 1989.

Brown, MacAlister, and Joseph J. Zasloff. *Cambodia Confounds the Peacemakers, 1979–1998.* Ithaca, N.Y.: Cornell University Press, 1998.

Brzezinski, Zbigniew. *Power and Principle: Memoirs of the National Security Adviser, 1977–1981.* New York: Farrar, Straus, and Giroux, 1983.

Bush, George, and Brent Scowcroft. *A World Transformed.* New York: Alfred A. Knopf, 1998.

Cambodia: An Australian Peace Proposal, Working Papers Prepared for the Informal Meeting on Cambodia, Jakarta, 26–28 February 1990. Canberra, Australia: Department of Foreign Affairs and Trade, 1990.

Chanda, Nayan. *Brother Enemy: The War after the War.* New York: Collier Books, 1986.

Chandler, David P. *The Tragedy of Cambodian History: Politics, War, and Revolution since 1945.* New Haven, Conn.: Yale University Press, 1991.

Childress, Richard T., and Stephen J. Solarz. "Vietnam: Detours on the Road to Normalization." In *Reversing Relations with Former Adversaries: U.S. Foreign Policy after the Cold War,* ed. C. Richard Nelson and Kenneth Weisbrode. Gainesville: University of Florida Press, 1998.

Crowley, Monica. *Nixon in Winter.* New York: Random House, 1998.

Doyle, Michael W. *UN Peacekeeping in Cambodia: UNTAC's Civil Mandate.* London and Boulder, Colo.: Lynne Rienner Publishers/International Peace Academy, 1995.

Elleman, Bruce. "Sino-Soviet Relations and the February 1979 Sino-Vietnamese Conflict." Paper presented at the Center for the Study of the Vietnam Conflict, Texas Tech University, Lubbock, April 17–20, 1996.

Evans, Gareth. *Cooperating for Peace: The Global Agenda for the 1990s and Beyond.* St. Leonards, Australia: Allen and Unwin, 1993.

Evans, Gareth, and Bruce Grant. *Australia's Foreign Relations in the World of the 1990s.* Melbourne, Australia: Melbourne University Press, 1991, 1995.

Findlay, Trevor. *Cambodia: The Legacy and Lessons of UNTAC.* SIPRI Research Report no. 9. Oxford, England: Oxford University Press, 1995.

Gorbachev, Mikhail S. *Memoirs.* New York: Doubleday, 1995.

———. *A Time for Peace.* New York: Richardson and Steinman, 1985.

Hampson, Fen Osler. *Nurturing Peace: Why Peace Settlements Succeed or Fail.* Washington, D.C.: United States Institute of Peace Press, 1996.

Hiebert, Murray. *Cambodia: Perspectives on the Impasse.* Washington, D.C.: Center for International Policy, February–March, 1986.

Kamm, Henry. *Cambodia: Report from a Stricken Land.* New York: Arcade Publishing, 1998.

Karnow, Stanley. *Vietnam: A History.* New York: Penguin Books, 1997.

Kiernan, Ben. *The Pol Pot Regime: Race, Power and Genocide in Cambodia under the Khmer Rouge, 1975–79.* New Haven, Conn.: Yale University Press, 1996.

Kissinger, Henry A. *White House Years.* Boston: Little, Brown, 1979.

———. *Years of Renewal.* New York: Simon and Schuster, 1999.

———. *Years of Upheaval.* Boston: Little, Brown, 1982.

Kohno, Masaharu. *In Search of Proactive Diplomacy: Increasing Japan's Diplomatic Role in the 1990s.* Washington, D.C.: Brookings Institution, Center for Northeast Asian Policy Studies, Working Paper Series, 1999.

Macchiarola, Frank J., and Robert B. Oxnam. *The China Challenge: American Policies in East Asia.* New York: Proceedings of the Academy of Political Science/The Asia Society 38, no. 2, 1991.

McNamara, Robert S. *In Retrospect: The Tragedy and Lessons of Vietnam.* New York: Random House, Times Books, 1996.

Peou, Sorpong. *Conflict Neutralization in the Cambodia War: From Battlefield to Ballot-box.* Kuala Lumpur: Malaysia: Oxford University Press, 1997.

Ratner, Steven R. "The Cambodia Settlement Agreements." *American Journal of International Law* 87, no. 1 (January 1993): 1–41.

Scott, Keith. *Gareth Evans.* St. Leonards, Australia: Allen and Unwin, 1999.

Shawcross, William. *Cambodia's New Deal.* Washington, D.C.: Carnegie Endowment for International Peace, 1994.

Shevardnadze, Eduard. *The Future Belongs to Freedom.* New York: Macmillan, 1991.

Shultz, George P. *Turmoil and Triumph: My Years as Secretary of State.* New York: Charles Scribner's Sons, 1993.

Solarz, Stephen J. "Cambodia and the International Community." *Foreign Affairs* 69, no. 2 (spring 1990): 99–115.

Sutter, Robert G. "America and the Cambodian Peace Agreement." In *The Diplomatic Record, 1991–1992,* ed. Binnendijk and Locke, Boulder, Colo.: Westview Press, 1993.

Thayer, Nate. *Sympathy for the Devil: Living Dangerously in Cambodia, a Foreign Correspondent's Story.* New York: Viking Press, 1999.

Index

Cambodia's King Sihanouk receives Richard Solomon at the royal palace in Phnom Penh in 1996, on the fifth anniversary of the signing of the Paris Peace Accords on Cambodia.

Richard H. Solomon has been president of the United States Institute of Peace since 1993. He served as assistant secretary of state for East Asian and Pacific affairs from 1989 to 1992, during which time he led U.S. negotiations for a Cambodian peace process and the development of an approach to normalizing relations with Vietnam. For his efforts he received awards from the U.S. Department of State, the Cambodian community in the United States, and the Government of Thailand.

Solomon's other assignments in the U.S. government have included ambassador to the Philippines (1992–93), director of the State Department's policy planning staff (1986–89), and senior staff member of the National Security Council (1971–76). He was head of the social science department at the RAND Corporation between 1976 and 1986, and professor of political science at the University of Michigan between 1966 and 1971. He holds a Ph.D. in political science from the Massachusetts Institute of Technology.

United States Institute of Peace

The United States Institute of Peace is an independent, nonpartisan federal institution created by Congress to promote research, education, and training on the peaceful management and resolution of international conflicts. Established in 1984, the Institute meets its congressional mandate through an array of programs, including research grants, fellowships, professional training, education programs from high school through graduate school, conferences and workshops, library services, and publications. The Institute's Board of Directors is appointed by the President of the United States and confirmed by the Senate.